HE TECH SET

ssa Kroski, Series Editor

#

9

Gaming
in Libraries

Kelly Nicole Czarnecki

Neal-Schuman Publishers, Inc.

New York London

Published by Neal-Schuman Publishers, Inc.
100 William St., Suite 2004
New York, NY 10038

Published in cooperation with the Library Information and Technology Association, a division of the American Library Association.

Figures 2.4–2.7 and 4.1 appear courtesy of the Charlotte Mecklenburg Library and are used by permission of Charles Brown, Director of Libraries.

Printed and bound in the United States of America.

The paper used in this publication meets the minimum requirements of American National Standard for Information Sciences—Permanence of Paper for Printed Library Materials, ANSI Z39.48-1992.

ISBN: 978-1-55570-709-5

CONTENTS

Don't miss this book's companion wiki and podcast!

Turn the page for details.

THE TECH SET is more than the book you're holding!

All 10 titles in THE TECH SET series feature three components:

1. the book you're now holding;
2. companion wikis to provide even more details on the topic and keep our coverage of this topic up-to-date; and
3. author podcasts that will extend your knowledge and let you get to know the author even better.

The companion wikis and podcasts can be found at:

techset.wetpaint.com

At **techset.wetpaint.com** you'll be able to go far beyond the printed pages you're now holding and:

▶ access regular updates from each author that are packed with new advice and recommended resources;
▶ use the wiki's forum to interact, ask questions, and share advice with the authors and your LIS peers; and
▶ hear these gurus' own words when you listen to THE TECH SET podcasts.

To receive regular updates about TECH SET technologies and authors, sign up for THE TECH SET Facebook page (**facebook.com/ nealschumanpub**) and Twitter (**twitter.com/nealschumanpub**).

For more information on THE TECH SET series and the individual titles, visit **www.neal-schuman.com/techset**.

▶

FOREWORD

Welcome to volume 9 of The Tech Set.

From modern board and card games to computer and online diversions to console entertainment, gaming is big in libraries. In *Gaming in Libraries*, author Kelly Czarnecki instructs readers about the ins and outs of setting up an innovative gaming program in your library that will have patrons of all types eager to participate. This comprehensive guide reveals how to host events such as a *Guitar Hero* fest, a *Magic: The Gathering* tournament, and a board game event and steps readers through the process of planning and implementing an appropriate program for their library. Readers will also garner game collection development tips, circulation best practices, and practical advice for facilitating tournaments. Whether you're planning a gaming program to introduce students to library resources or to host an anime fest, this is the ultimate field guide.

The idea for The Tech Set book series developed because I perceived a need for a set of practical guidebooks for using today's cutting-edge technologies specifically within libraries. When I give talks and teach courses, what I hear most from librarians who are interested in implementing these new tools in their organizations are questions on how exactly to go about doing it. A lot has been written about the benefits of these new 2.0 social media tools, and at this point librarians are intrigued but they oftentimes don't know where to start.

I envisioned a series of books that would offer accessible, practical information and would encapsulate the spirit of a 23 Things program but go a step further—to teach librarians not only how to use these programs as individual users but also how to plan and implement particular types of library services using them. I thought it was important to discuss the entire life cycle of these initiatives, including everything from what it takes to plan, strategize, and gain buy-in, to how to develop and implement, to how to market and measure the success of these projects. I also wanted them to incorporate a broad range of project ideas and instructions.

Each of the ten books in The Tech Set series was written with this format in mind. Throughout the series, the "Implementation" chapters, chock-full of detailed project instructions, will be of major interest to all readers. These chapters start off with a basic "recipe" for how to effectively use the technology in a library and then build on that foundation to offer more and more advanced project ideas. I believe that readers of all levels of expertise will find something useful here as the proposed projects and initiatives run the gamut from the basic to the cutting-edge.

Kelly Czarnecki has been writing and speaking about gaming in libraries for years. After reading her "Gaming Life" column in *School Library Journal*, I knew that Kelly would excel at writing a gaming book specifically geared toward librarians. And she did. If you're thinking about implementing a gaming program in your library, this is a must-read resource.

Ellyssa Kroski
Information Services Technologist
Barnard College Library
www.ellyssakroski.com
http://oedb.org/blogs/ilibrarian
ellyssakroski@yahoo.com

Ellyssa Kroski is an Information Services Technologist at Barnard College as well as a writer, educator, and international conference speaker. She is an adjunct faculty member at Long Island University, Pratt Institute, and San Jose State University where she teaches LIS students about emerging technologies. Her book *Web 2.0 for Librarians and Information Professionals* was published in February 2008, and she is the creator and Series Editor for The Tech Set 10-volume book series. She blogs at iLibrarian and writes a column called "Stacking the Tech" for *Library Journal*'s Academic Newswire.

▶

PREFACE

Many people think video games like *Grand Theft Auto* promote violent behavior in children. Other critics believe video games are a major cause of obesity. Some librarians haven't introduced gaming in their libraries because they believe video games are incompatible with the library's mission and they fear gaming will encourage disruptive behavior. This negativity about gaming has caused both schools and libraries to miss tremendous opportunities to foster literacy development, new avenues for socialization, and increased library usage.

Even gaming's critics will agree with two assertions:

▶ Children, teens, and adults love to play games whether it is checkers, chess, card games, or video games.
▶ Gaming is not just a passing fad.

Because we know these two things, it makes sense to learn how to use gaming effectively to attract people to the library and all its riches. Toward this end, *Gaming in Libraries* introduces the latest in gaming technology.

To succeed at any game, gamers must engage search strategies and critical thinking skills. Gaming provides a combination of face-to-face and digital interaction that opens up social connections that were previously never possible. Gaming has evolved into a global social activity, with online play among libraries. It has also gone mobile, scaling down with an ever-increasing number of games available for handheld devices. According to a report by the Entertainment Software Association (www.theesa.com/facts/pdfs/

ESA_EF_2009.pdf), the average age of a gamer is 35. Because gaming has a great ability to bring people from all walks of life together and through different mediums, video games offer much to academic, public, and school libraries of all sizes.

▶ ORGANIZATION AND AUDIENCE

Gaming in Libraries is designed to be a practical, step-by-step guide for all librarians wanting to develop gaming tournaments and circulating games collection and to bring gaming programs to the library. Chapter 1 provides a basic introduction to the latest in gaming platforms, consoles, and devices libraries can utilize in developing gaming programs. Chapter 2 covers things to consider when planning a gaming program, including costs and funding, getting buy-in from staff, and developing a game space. Chapter 3 covers how to implement different gaming programs, such as a monthly video game tournament, a board game event, and hosting a Guitar Hero Fest. Chapter 4 covers how to market a new gaming program, while Chapter 5 discusses gaming best practices. Chapter 6 looks at different ways you can measure the success of your gaming program. A resources section covering emerging trends and additional material on gaming in libraries is included at the end of the book.

Gaming in Libraries provides librarians with the skills necessary to develop a gaming program that fosters critical thinking skills, new ways of socialization, and literacy. If you're new to gaming, read this book, but don't hesitate to put it down and try the games that interest you. You'll learn something and even enjoy it.

▶1

INTRODUCTION: GAMING OPTIONS AND IDEAS

▶ Gaming Consoles, Platforms, and Devices
▶ Ideas for Use

Video game playing is not just kids play. According the Entertainment Software Association (ESA; www.theesa.com), 68 percent of American households play computer or video games, with the average game player being 35 years old. The video game market represents a huge branch of the technology industry in America and is a major economic indicator, with 297.6 million video games being sold in 2008 (www.theesa.com/gamesindailylife/families.pdf, accessed November 2009). Some of these data may seem surprising, but libraries should embrace them when it comes time to decide on whether developing a video game collection or gaming service for their library is appropriate. One fact that has always been true is that kids love to play games. Gaming in libraries provides an opportunity to draw kids into a book-rich environment to learn and, of course, have fun.

▶ GAMING CONSOLES, PLATFORMS, AND DEVICES

In this section I will introduce you to the major consoles and platforms for games, what they're mostly used for in libraries, as well as upcoming trends (see Figure 1.1).

Nintendo Wii

Over 50 million Nintendo Wii consoles have been sold worldwide. Many libraries have purchased the Wii because of its somewhat low

▶ Figure 1.1: Next-Generation Consoles: (From left to right) Nintendo Wii, PlayStation 3, and Xbox 360

cost ($199.00 since the price drop in September 2009 and still currently cheaper than the Xbox 360 and PlayStation 3) and because it reaches across boundaries of who plays video games. MotionPlus controls, a peripheral that attaches to the Wiimote (the primary controller used with the Wii console), were released in June 2009. The MotionPlus detects the rate of rotation or the direction the Wiimote is pointing with a lot better accuracy in motion sensing during game play. *Wii Sports Resort*, a sequel to *Wii Sports*, comes with one Wii MotionPlus control and includes games such as *Table Tennis, Frisbee, Power Cruising* and *Air Sports* such as *Hang Gliding*. While libraries don't necessarily have to upgrade their Wii, you probably can't go wrong because *Wii Sports* is popular in many libraries. Another game for the Wii is *Super Mario Brothers*, which was released in late 2009. This is the first version to allow multiple players at the same time, a plus for libraries. While it might seem sometimes that consoles are always changing too fast to keep up with them, you can easily get well over five years of a marketable life out of the systems, especially because most of the games are backward compatible (older games able to play on newer systems).

Microsoft Xbox 360

The price of the Xbox 360 console dropped to $300.00 in fall 2009. Project Natal, a full-body game control system announced at E3 2009, is expected to come out for the Xbox 360 sometime in 2010. It allows for controller-free gaming and play based on the movements of the body. Facial and voice recognition are also used to play the games. For demonstration videos, see www.gametrailers .com/video/e3-09-project-natal/50013 (accessed 2009).

According to Wikipedia, "The Electronic Entertainment Expo," commonly known as E3, is an annual trade show for the computer and video games industry presented by the Entertainment Software Association (ESA). It is used by many video game developers to show off their upcoming games and game-related hardware (http://en .wikipedia.org/wiki/E3_Expo, accessed January 2009).

Sony PlayStation 3

The price for the PlayStation 3 (PS3) console is $299.00 for 120 GB and $349.00 for 250 GB. The new PS3 Slim came out in late summer 2009 and is more energy efficient and lighter in weight. The motion controller, due out in spring 2010 (announced at E3), works by having the PS Eye camera track the wand, which looks like a purple ball sitting atop a stick. The PlayStation Eye along with EyeCreate software also functions as video editing software where video, audio, and photos can be captured and edited into a movie.

Here are some video games for multiple platforms that libraries may want to be aware of because of their ability to bring diverse ages together with strong literacy tie-ins:

▶ *Beatles Rock Band* for Wii, PS3, and Xbox 360. Libraries that host intergenerational gaming programs may be interested in purchasing a copy. Players have 45 songs from the Beatles to choose from. Rated T for Teen.

▶ *Guitar Hero 5* for Wii, PS3 and PS2, Xbox 360, and Nintendo DS. Unlike *Guitar Hero World Tour*, in *GH 5*, all four players can play the same instrument if they choose. Otherwise, players can choose vocals, drums, and lead or bass guitar. Rated T for Teen.

▶ *Batman: Arkham Asylum* for PS3, Xbox 360, and PC. Batman must put an end to the Joker's plans, which involves creating an army of inmates to help him. Rated T for Teen.

▶ *Star Wars: The Clone Wars: Republic Heroes* for Wii, PC, PS2 and PS3, Xbox 360, PSP, and Nintendo DS, released in October 2009. Like the popular TV series, players can continue the storyline by fighting as a Jedi and clone trooper in over 30 missions. Rated T for Teen and E10+ for Everyone age ten and older for DS.

▶ *Professor Layton and the Diabolical Box* for Nintendo DS. Engaging riddles and brainteasers that the Professor and his apprentice Luke encounter as they try to solve the overarching mystery. Dr. Schrader, the Professor's mentor, is found dead, and no one knows why. Rated E10+ for Everyone age ten and older.

Keep in mind that the Wii, PS3, and Xbox 360 all connect to the Internet, which means libraries can purchase games online and use the connecting capabilities and profile creation tools to make communities to promote events and services. Downloadable games are reviewed in most major gaming magazines listed in the Recommended Reading section at the end of this book.

Computers: PCs and Macs

Streaming browser-based video games such as *OnLive* (www.onlive .com, accessed 2009) announced at the 2009 Game Developers Conference, or *Gaikai* (gaikai.com, accessed 2009), are new, up-and-coming games for PCs and Macs, allowing users to play without downloads, installs, or updates. With the purchase of a MicroConsole, which can be connected to a television, the same service can be offered to those who don't have a computer.

Netbooks, which retail for under $400.00, are lightweight laptop computers. They run basic browser-based online games, game creation software, or virtual worlds such as Small Worlds (www .smallworlds.com, accessed 2009) or Webkinz (www.webkinz.com, accessed 2009).

Handhelds and Mobile Devices

GoKnow! software developer Elliot Soloway states that, "The future is mobile devices that are connected. They're going to be the new paper and pencil" (www.ns.umich.edu/htdocs/releases/story .php?id=6976, accessed 2009). While some universities and school districts have adopted using handheld devices such as cell phones as learning tools for creating animations and other applications, the norm is that these devices are seen as a distraction and not taken seriously.

In June 2009, the Joan Ganz Cooney Center at Sesame Street Workshop published a report, "Pockets of Potential: Using Mobile

Technologies to Promote Children's Learning" (www.joanganz cooneycenter.org/pdf/pockets_of_potential.pdf, accessed 2009). The report describes the global successes of projects designed to explore the learning potential of such mobile devices as cell phones, iPods, and gaming platforms.

The Mobile Gaming Resource Center is a great site for information on mobile gaming articles, tutorials, and more (www.deitel.com/ ResourceCenters/GamesandGameProgramming/MobileGaming /tabid/2446/Default.aspx, accessed 2009).

Sony PlayStation Portable

The PlayStation Portable (PSP) Go is Sony's latest version of its handheld device, released in October 2009. It has built-in Wi-Fi and memory to store games and other media. Libraries that already have the previous version of the PSP probably don't need to upgrade. If it is an option, work with IT so that all handhelds can connect to the Internet without interfering with the normal traffic of computer use.

Nintendo DSi and DS

The DSi, which was preceded by the DS Lite, became available in spring 2009. Most DS games are compatible with the DSi. Downloadable games are available. More than just a gaming system, it can store, modify, upload, and take photos; act as a voice recorder; and connect to the Internet. *Guitar Hero 5* has an application for the Nintendo DS that creates the ability to sabotage the opposing guitarist who is playing on the Wii at the same time.

GPS Units

Global positioning systems (GPSs) are handheld units that can be rented or purchased used or new from around $10.00 to $50.00 (they can also cost hundreds of dollars). The Geospatial Information and Technology Association, or GITA (www.gita.org, accessed 2009), has a Location in Education program (http://gita.org/resources/location_in_education/loc-in-edu.asp, accessed 2009) whereby educators can rent units for a deposit fee of $50.00. GPS units can be used for geocaching, which is an outdoor scavenger hunt based on finding objects using longitude and latitude coordinates. Many alternate reality games (ARGs) integrate geocaching.

Cell Phones and iPods

According to *Library Journal* blogger Liz Danforth, it is important for libraries to recognize and incorporate mobile devices because they are a significant way that many patrons access their information (www.libraryjournal.com/blog/1130000713/post/1840048784 .html, accessed 2009). While iPods are generally used for storing and playing music, they can also store games, of which there are currently over 21,000 titles. Similarly, many cell phones and personal digital assistants (PDAs), such as the BlackBerry, support games. Some of the most popular games for cell phones and PDAs are *Tetris* and *Sudoku.*

▶ IDEAS FOR USE

This book covers a wide range of hands-on activities and services that libraries—school, public, and academic—can institute with gaming. Libraries celebrate National Gaming Day in November, and this is a perfect time to introduce people to not only how to play certain games but also how to find other related resources at the library.

People like to compete against one another, and gaming is a perfect opportunity to do so. Many video, card, and board games lend themselves well to tournaments. Open play allows people from all ages, including young and older adults, to play with their children, grandchildren, and other youth they help mentor, and is a great activity that transgresses boundaries more so than other library activities. There's no limit to tying gaming into the curriculum or a gaming-related career with the services that libraries have to offer. Hopefully you'll pick up some ideas and connections with gaming and libraries you hadn't thought about before and share them with others!

►2

PLANNING

- ► Plan for Costs and Funding
- ► Develop Game Spaces and Programs
- ► Get Staff Involved
- ► Focus on Program Specifics
- ► Plan a Circulating Game Collection
- ► Create Program Forms

Implementing gaming programs and gaming as a service in a library, no matter how large or small, isn't always an easy feat. You may look at what other libraries all around the country are doing with gaming and think, "Why can't we do that too?" or "Why haven't we been doing that for years?" Well, you can, and this book is going to show you how. This chapter offers many tips on how to plan your gaming program.

► PLAN FOR COSTS AND FUNDING

Cost is often a large factor in a library's decision to support gaming as a service, as systems and games are expensive and can become outdated fairly quickly. You might think if the library can't keep up to some extent, what benefit would gaming offer in the first place? Remember, though, as Scordato (2008: 69) points out, "After an initial investment, equipment can be used repeatedly. Similar to storytime materials such as puppets and props, video game consoles and games can be reused, whereas craft activities entail supplies that need refreshing." Here are some ways that your library can keep up and plan for the costs of establishing a gaming program.

Apply for a Grant

Many libraries have obtained grant funding to introduce their gaming program with a big splash. For example, the Carvers Bay Branch at the Georgetown County Library in South Carolina (www.gclibrary.org, accessed 2009) implemented an interactive computer gaming center for teens in conjunction with the goal of developing a habit of using the library regularly. The funding for the center came from a Frances P. Bunnelle grant (www.bunnelle .org, accessed 2009), which was available just for that county, and exemplifies how to address the cost, space, IT, and literacy issues.

The Columbus Metropolitan Library Board of trustees approved over $40,000.00 in 2007 for the purchase of game equipment (PS2 and Wii consoles and games) for its library system. More than 20,000 teens attended the gaming programs at Columbus Metropolitan Library (www.columbuslibrary.org, accessed 2009) at the end of eight weeks of summer reading. I mention these two programs because it can help you imagine what is possible at your own library.

Often local organizations such as the Rotary Club and Junior League, stores such as Walmart and Best Buy, or your state library will offer funding opportunities. Don't dismiss a grant just because it doesn't specifically state it is for gaming or for the exact gaming console you had in mind. Think outside of the box when searching for connections among gaming and literacy, education, or healthy communities. Networking with members in the community can also introduce you to other funding opportunities that might be available. Talking with people at libraries that have received grants for gaming may help you develop a game funding idea. In spring 2010, the American Library Association and Verizon Foundation awarded ten libraries funding to develop new and original gaming programs (follow their progress at www.librarygamingtoolkit.org, accessed 2009).

The following list includes organizations and grants that you might consider applying for in relation to your gaming program. While some of the grants might appear as more of a direct fit, libraries and similar organizations have received funding from many of them for gaming and game-related projects:

▶ **Advanced Micro Devices, Inc. (AMD) Foundation**: Changing the Game (www.amd.com/us-en/0,,3715_14217_15653_15654,00 .html, accessed 2009)

▶ **Association for Library Service to Children (ALSC)/Candlewick Press**: Light the Way: Outreach to the Underserved (www .ala.org/ala/mgrps/divs/alsc/awardsgrants/profawards/candle wicklighttheway/index.cfm, accessed 2009)

▶ **Funagain Games**: Monthly Game Grants (www.funagain.com/ control/rc?p=grants, accessed 2009)

▶ **Humanities, Arts, Science, and Technology Advanced Collaboratory (HASTAC)**: Digital Media and Learning Initiative (www.dmlcompetition.net, accessed 2009)

▶ **Institute of Museum and Library Services (IMLS)** (www.imls .gov/applicants/applicants.shtm, accessed 2009)

▶ **Library Services and Technology Act (LSTA)** (varies by state)

▶ **National Council on Aging** (www.ncoa.org, accessed 2009)

▶ **Robert Wood Johnson Foundation** (www.rwjf.org/grants, accessed 2009)

▶ **Verizon Foundation** (http://foundation.verizon.com/grant/ guidelines.shtml, accessed 2009)

▶ **Wallace Foundation** (www.wallacefoundation.org/Grants Programs/Pages, accessed 2009)

▶ **Young Adult Library Services Association (YALSA)**: Teen Tech Week Mini Grants (www.ala.org/ala/mgrps/divs/yalsa/teen techweek/ttw09/home.cfm, accessed 2009)

Create/Design Your Own Games

Gaming doesn't require you to buy equipment that costs several hundred dollars. You can create and play your own games on a number of free Web sites, such as Game Maker (www.yoyogames .com, accessed 2009), Scratch (www.scratch.mit.edu, accessed 2009), Cube (www.cubeengine.com, accessed 2009), Byond (www.byond .com, accessed 2009), and Gamestar Mechanic (www.gamestar me-chanic.com, accessed 2009).

Learning game design can be a great parent/child activity and start of a career path as well. For a more comprehensive list of game design programs, check out the August 2009 issue of *PC Gamer* (www.pcgamer.com, accessed 2009). It is a special edition issue called "Big Book of the Free" and lists over 365 free games, including game design software.

Partner with Local Organizations

Partnering with local organizations for gaming can mean more than just with a local game store. Places such as parks and recreation centers will likely have the audience and the space you may need. Since 2005, this is what the Bloomington Public Library in Illinois has been doing (http://www.bngamefest.org/, accessed 2009). A senior center will likely welcome the physical and mental activities gaming can provide for the residents.

Science fiction or anime conventions will likely more than welcome libraries to demonstrate their services for fans. Send an e-mail via their Web site's Contact Us page for the event to get the ball rolling. Check out what the Wake County Libraries in North Carolina are doing at Animazement (www.animazement.org, accessed 2009), an annual anime/manga convention in Raleigh (http://yalsa.ala.org/blog/2009/05/25/how-to-sponsor-a-manga-library-at-an-anime-con, accessed 2009).

Museums can also be key partners in gaming initiatives. The Hennepin County Library (www.hclib.org, accessed 2009) and the Science Museum of Minnesota (www.smm.org, accessed 2009) have a long-term partnership based on developing twenty-first-century skills and game design. School counselors, colleges, and gaming companies can also help provide great resources for those considering a career in gaming. There's no limit to the angles with gaming that partnerships can help play a role in.

Shop for Used Games and Equipment

Don't forget about used games and consoles, which can be found at most gaming stores. Libraries often have a "food for fines" day. Perhaps bringing in gently used video or board games in exchange for fines would interest patrons. Many gaming programs at libraries begin with staff members bringing in their equipment to start building a case for the library to put real funding into the program. Gaming stores themselves might be interested in donating and setting up equipment once a month to help support your library. It's a win–win for both sides. Game consoles and games can also be rented from most places where movies can be rented. See what you can find, but don't forget to ask your patrons what they would want. Tapping into their needs might lead you to some deals and bargains you never thought about before.

▶ DEVELOP GAME SPACES AND PROGRAMS

Finding an adequate space in the library for games can be a challenge, particularly because of the noise the participants can make when playing (think of how loud storytime can get, and then multiply by ten). This is especially true if the games are music oriented, such as *Rock Band* and *Guitar Hero.*

Establish Separate Spaces

If you are in the position of having your library remodeled, consider advocating for a gaming space, preferably enclosed to allow for noise, that would more freely support the needs of all kinds of games. A mobile computer area that doesn't interfere with the needs of patrons trying to access homework or a class is always a plus.

The McCracken County Public Library (www.mclib.net, accessed 2009) in Kentucky sports what it calls the YAM Bar (Young Adult Media Bar) where PlayStation 2s and about 20 video games are available to anyone for play. "Normal teenage behavior is expected," which means that noise is tolerated. They post explicit rules on their Web site and in the gaming area itself of what is not allowed (www.mclib.net/teenyam.html, accessed 2009). If an entire space dedicated to gaming is just way too ambitious (or is not within your library's budget), here are some alternatives:

- ▶ Develop a partnership with an organization that could support the noise level and space needs.
- ▶ Hold an after-hours program so that the noise doesn't interfere with other services during the day.
- ▶ Let patrons know well in advance not to expect a quiet building during certain hours on a certain date for when the program is scheduled.
- ▶ Establish regular gaming hours such as after school or on weekends so that people will know what to expect in terms of the space and activity.

Go Outside

A space for gaming could even be the outdoor area surrounding your library. There is a genre of games called Big Games (http://gaming.techsource.ala.org/index.php/Big_Fun%2C_Big_Learning:_Transforming_the_World_through_Play, accessed 2009) in which entire city blocks are literally used as the game board. Talk about partnerships! Ravenchase Adventures, based in Virginia (www.ravenchase.com, accessed 2009) is a good example of what games that take place across the city might involve.

As mentioned in Chapter 1, geocaching involves a GPS unit, similar to the units in cars that give directions. GPS units are also handheld devices that are used for walking and hiking to find hidden treasures. Geocaching usually takes place outdoors and can be transformed into a type of Big Game. Visit www.geocaching.com (accessed 2009) for tips on how it works.

Transform Existing Programs

The library's summer reading program can be thought of as a type of game (i.e., read so many books and win a prize), so in a sense we already are using the library to offer gaming as a service. Sometimes the themes easily lend themselves to incorporate games, such as the Illinois 2009 program "Get in the Game: READ!" (www.alia.org.au/src/resource_man.pdf, accessed 2009). Also, many books nowadays are adaptable because they are directly about characters in games or may require the reader to use the Internet in order to interact with the story.

For more on transforming existing programs into gaming opportunities for young adult readers, see Lindsay Wesson and Lori Easterwood's article in *School Library Journal*, "Gamers Are Readers: Capitalize on the Popularity of Video Games" (www.schoollibraryjournal.com/article/CA6647714.html, accessed 2009).

Repackaging to capitalize on the game-playing aspects of familiar and routine services might draw in more people to participate in those services. Furthermore, many positive learning outcomes are a result of gaming, and promoting learning is what libraries are all about.

▶ GET STAFF INVOLVED

Coordinate with IT

If your library has an information technology department, it's important to work with its staff to help meet your gaming needs. At the very least, they should be aware of the library offering gaming as a service, especially if there are opportunities such as meetings or conversations where this information can be shared. If they're in the know, they will be more likely to be on board when you need their assistance, such as when installing online games, connecting handhelds to the library's Wi-Fi, or making a port live so that you can engage in online gaming with another library.

They may also be great allies for gaming and able to give advice on what games and equipment to purchase. Not all of our involvement with IT needs to be an exchange of, "Can you do this for me?" They can be great resources and would probably appreciate a little time away from fixing things to show off their skills at racing a car or fighting an enemy on the screen.

Working with the IT department to offer gaming as a service, especially if it's at the scale of having a large dedicated and permanent space, will require time and understanding on both ends. While many of the IT staff might be gamers themselves, don't assume that they necessarily make all the connections among gaming, learning, and literacy in their own minds. Is that necessary for them to do so just because you want the latest version of Google SketchUp (http://sketchup.google.com, accessed 2009) installed on your computers? In a way, yes. Their time is money and important just like yours is. Sometimes the person making the requests and the IT staff are juggling two hats at once and must choose their priorities. While it might not be your responsibility to design the structure for making requests from IT, if you feel things could flow more smoothly in getting things done, particularly in relation to gaming, by all means suggest a more formalized process. If installation is involved, suggest a timetable when that could be done, or offer alternative suggestions such as installing it yourself on a flash drive and then running it on a networked computer.

Whether these needs are a priority will depend on a lot of different factors at your organization.

Know Your Stuff!

Be able to answer questions about what games have to do with libraries, literacy, and learning in a clear and understandable way, especially to nongamers. This will help in the long run to clear some of the paths for you to be able to implement gaming.

Besides, once you have buy-in for offering gaming, you will have another rich resource of people who will be a huge asset in helping get the word out as to why the library is supporting this activity. Again, you will be the best judge of the climate of your library's community in where to start with gaming.

The American Library Association's online gaming toolkit (http://librarygamingtoolkit.org/, accessed 2009) includes a comprehensive discussion of the relationship between gaming and literacy, and best practices are linked with relationships to literacy. Also, the Board Games and AASL Standards for the 21st-Century Learner is a helpful document that makes the case for gaming related to the curriculum (http://sls.gvboces.org/gaming /sites/sls.gvboces.org.gaming/files/Story%20Documents/ aaslgamealignment(sheets).pdf, accessed 2009).

Make Your Case

The goals for your program or service should determine what approach you take when making your case about gaming. For example, if the obesity rate is really high in your community, the purchase of a game that involves a lot of physical activity would not only be an opportunity to introduce fun, physical activities to people but also teach people about health and physical well-being. Partnerships with parks and recreation centers, as well as physical fitness experts within the community, could help bolster the message that games promoting physical education and movement are fun, new, and exciting ways to help overweight people.

If test scores are low for a particular age group and subject, investing in some Wii games such as *Brain Age* (www.brainage.com, accessed 2009) might give a great supplemental context to learning.

Trivia and puzzle games can provide players with knowledge they didn't have before starting the game. And because the knowledge delivery vehicle is a game and not an actual classroom, some kids will be more receptive and better able to retain the information.

Another selling point for developing a gaming program is creation of an environment where people who might not otherwise socialize with each other come together and discover new cultures, people, and resources they never expected to find at the library. This kind of approach seems to work especially well in academic libraries. The socialization connection happens often with gaming, and participants are likely to see the library facility with fresh eyes because it implemented a service directly relevant to them. When Ed McDonald, a librarian at the Charlotte Mecklenburg Library, coordinated a systemwide Madden football tournament for all ages in 2009, he found that not only did participants come from a variety of cultures but many were also first-time library visitors. Undoubtedly, several of them learned that the library can be a place that promotes acceptance and will return to the library and continue discovering information that suits their needs.

▶ FOCUS ON PROGRAM SPECIFICS

If you have had success in purchasing the equipment, finding space for your program or service, working with IT, and/or connecting libraries with gaming through literacy and learning, you are ready to move forward with your plan. Depending on how involved it is, it might be a good idea to keep a checklist or use a wiki to record the details of making it all happen, as well as a "things to keep in mind for next time" list. This way you won't have to reinvent the wheel or forget things. Your program may involve more staff than just you. Try to plan enough in advance to get other staff to commit their time with helping out. Especially if it's the first time for running a gaming program, it might be better to have a few extra on board if possible. If you're working with outside partners or a Teen Advisory Board, many of them will be able to serve in a capacity similar to staff.

Develop or Tweak Policies

Don't be afraid to examine your current policies around gaming as the service develops. At my library, we have a lot of youth under 12 (we define teens as ages 12 through 18) wanting to play T-rated (Teen) games. We decided with parental permission to allow this, and we note it on their library card record. We also changed the amount of time they could game in the summer during our busiest times from 30 minutes to a full hour so that the increased scheduling demands on staff doing programs and handling large amounts of people would not become prohibitive.

Involve your patrons in determining some of the procedures, such as, how long is a fair amount of time for people to play? How do people sign up? What is fair for tournament rules? Chances are that the participants will be more invested if they get to help make the rules.

Also, your library likely already has policies for behavior and perhaps even for checking out board games. Don't think you have to completely reinvent the wheel in terms of these policies because video games might be new to your library. Start with what you already have and see how you can build off of them to address some of the areas you would like to with gaming. This chapter concludes with a few sample forms and policies for situations such as checking out materials to other branches within the system and allowing patrons to bring their own gaming equipment.

Record and Publish the Event

Follow your library's photo and video policies with regard to capturing mementos of the event. If you need permission to take photos and are able to get permission ahead of time, do so. Then it is time to put your photographic skills to work! Up-close shots, especially of a celebratory nature, are usually better than the backs of a group of people staring at the screen or a game board. Short videos that can capture the excitement in the room are even better.

If your library's policy on photos and videos is very restrictive but you're able to post quotes, even if anonymous after the event, gather up what you can and post them on your blog, Facebook, or other social networking site. Use quotes as part of your advertisement for the next event. Telling stories through anecdotes can go a long way to making a case as to how gaming and libraries are such a great fit. Librarian Aaron Schmidt captured quotes on the spot in 2005 (www.walkingpaper.org/267, accessed 2009) by making a laptop available during the event. While using the laptop for instant messaging didn't work that well, Schmidt still got quotes from the participants on his own. His favorite was, "Hey Aaron, can I go upstairs to grab a magazine and book to read?"

Control Loss and Damage

To help deter theft of materials, many libraries require users to have a library card before they can handle the equipment. Although this will exclude some from being able to play, it does give the library a way to help recover the cost of lost or stolen equipment. If possible, it is a good rule of thumb to budget extra money for equipment that might need to be replaced not only because of theft but also wear and tear over time. Don't be afraid to revise policies in order to cover a loss that you hadn't originally anticipated. Having staff be present at all times during an event will help lessen the chance that gaming equipment will walk out the door.

Reserve Equipment

You can probably never over plan when it comes to making sure you have met all your equipment needs. There is always the chance that being one power strip too short or two batteries undercharged will create disaster. While you'll learn as you go, you can certainly try to minimize the negative effects of poor planning by scheduling such things as a run-through before the actual event. Make sure you or someone else is comfortable with turning on the projector. Make sure the outlets you will be using are in working order. Reserve the equipment in plenty of time, and have some extra batteries on hand. We'll go over equipment more in depth in Chapter 3.

Publicize the Event

Most libraries have a standardized procedure for publicizing events. You've probably seen the results from program information being spread via word of mouth. Don't take this approach for granted—especially with gaming! While flyers and postings in your library's calendar will certainly attract attention, nothing can spread something faster than a peer telling one another what is happening at the library. Social networking sites such as Facebook or MySpace are great means of advertising. Ann Arbor Public Library uses a very interactive discussion board on its library site (www.aadl.org/aadlgt, accessed 2009) where trash talk (good-humored competitive joking around) abounds and comments are consistently left by participants—sometimes several hundred! Often, actual game play before the event is also a great way to advertise.

Gamers are happy to help unlock characters in a game for your event, which not only helps you but also helps others keep in the loop who might come by and ask what's going on. Making videos with the game characters to promo the event can also be a great way for the word to get out. Don't forget the forums for the actual game you might be playing. If your patrons are fans of *Super Smash Brothers*, you can bet they are cruising the Smash World Forums (www.smashboards.com, accessed 2009) regularly to see if there are any local events taking place (see Chapter 4 for more on marketing).

Award Prizes

When planning the event, you might want to consider giving prizes if you have the funding or a partner that may help. It's not necessary to have prizes, but they are a great incentive—especially gift certificates to gaming stores or, if you have a local gaming café, paid time there so your gamers can continue their experience at another venue. Sometimes library-related prizes, such as lowering fines, giving a coupon for extra time on the computers, or giving away galleys, are good alternatives.

▶ PLAN A CIRCULATING GAME COLLECTION

Many libraries offer gaming programs but may not circulate video games. Some libraries allow video games to be checked out by patrons but may not have gaming activities on a regular basis. Neither scenario is right or wrong. Circulating video games is first and foremost about your community and whether or not allowing this service will meet a need at your library and add value to your patrons' experiences.

Get Staff Buy-In

Finding out exactly how those responsible for collection development feel about adding video games to the library's collection is part of doing your homework to make your case. Promoting the potential benefits of a new gaming program is important. Here are some ideas on ways to get support for a new gaming collection.

Link Video Games with the Library's Mission

Take a look at your library's mission statement. Chances are that it includes something about being a "place for all," whether this is reflected in the library's resources and materials or in the library space itself. National reports and statistics about gamers (such as the Pew Internet & American Life Project at www.pewinternet.org) can help provide an understanding of the nature of the gaming population and why it might be important that your library address this by way of circulating games. Gather local statistics by conducting a poll of library and nonlibrary users. Make sure you have the necessary permission from your library before developing and executing such a questionnaire.

Address Funding Concerns

If there is a lot of resistance to spending taxpayer dollars on a collection that the library is not sure will ultimately be a good thing, you may want to seek out other resources besides monies from the budget to fund the collection. Donations, a Friends group, and grants through such places as the local Rotary Club are options. Consider presenting these alternatives as a pilot project. If circulating the collection has very positive outcomes for your library, perhaps looking at how budgetary funds can be put toward the video games at a later date would make more sense and be welcomed by the community once you have your data in place.

Describe the Effects of Circulating Video Games in the Library

While you may be putting together the information as to why it would be valuable for your library to start circulating video games, this definitely isn't a one-person show to help it run successfully. The bigger picture involves keeping the board and administration informed of the outcomes. Working with administrators to determine what aspects of impact are important to them in the first place will help you know where to shift your focus once the collection is in place. Looking at circulation and program statistics before the collection was added and comparing them with statistics gathered after will go a long way in determining if the service should continue. Anecdotes from patrons, positive and negative, will help provide a richer context for those questions that numbers alone can't adequately answer.

Identify the Myths about Video Games

The purpose of talking to patrons and library staff regarding their knowledge about video games isn't to expose anyone's ignorance but to identify what information may be missing or misinterpreted regarding the format. Knowing how much others know will help you determine where your presentation may need to focus to address concerns as well as what long-term commitment in educating others may be needed once the collection is kicked off the ground.

One stereotype you may encounter is that all video games have negative content, such as extreme violence. Belief that the collection would be stolen on a regular basis may be another. This can be addressed by looking at how other libraries adapted policies over time to combat theft of materials.

Develop Your Collection

While the staff ordering the games intended for circulation may not actually be deciding on which games to purchase, it is important to keep them involved in the decision-making process. Inviting them to any presentations you make, which ideally would touch upon points they have raised, is the best way to proceed.

The type of games you think the library should collect, whether for contemporary or vintage players, will factor into the budget in terms of storage and security. You'll want to include recommendations from patrons in your presentation to staff and include examples of the differences between a cartridge and a disc or CD-ROM (see Figure 2.1) and discuss what equipment is needed for each.

Specify genres you think the library should collect based on the expressed interests of the community. You can also suggest genres based on the library's target demographic. Sports, fantasy, music, racing, action/adventure, role playing, and family are common genres. Screenshots or demos of the actual games can give people a clearer idea of what exactly you are referring to. Relating your examples to who the collection is for (including how many can play at one time) is key in establishing a gaming service at your library.

Circulation data from libraries that have been circulating video games may show an increased number of books being checked out and an increased number of summer reading registrations after adding this new format to their collection. Both are statistics that will help dispel the myth that video games might not have anything to do with a library's mission. These kind of data can also be helpful in assuaging fears that if the library starts circulating video games it will become no different from an arcade at the mall. One way to identify which libraries are circulating video games is to visit

▶ Figure 2.1: Game CDs and Cartridges

the LibSuccess wiki (www.libsuccess.org/index.php?title=
Libraries_Circulating_Games, accessed 2009).

When your library made the decision to circulate graphic novels, music, or movies (while not all public libraries circulate these
items, most do), the arguments against doing this were probably
very similar to those given for why video games shouldn't be part of
the collection. It may be worth pointing out in your proposal the
parallels in terms of how all of these formats answer a community
interest as well as go hand in hand with other materials that
circulate in the collection.

In her book *Totally Wired: What Teens and Tweens Are Really Doing
Online,* Ypulse blogger and author Anastasia Goodstein (2007)
provides a great overview with a timeline of formats, accompanied
by anecdotes, that were looked down upon when they first hit the
scene, such as rock music, comics, and video games. You can use
excerpts of these anecdotes when you address the topic of circulating games at your library.

Consider Game Ratings, Consoles, and Content

The climate of your library administration and community, as well
as logistics like where you plan to shelve the games, will largely determine what ratings will be acceptable for purchase. Ratings are
given by the Entertainment Software Rating Board (www.esrb.org,
accessed 2009), which is a nonprofit and nongovernment-related
agency. The commercially licensed games your library will be purchasing will likely have been rated by the ESRB. The rating symbols are defined at www.esrb.org/ratings/ratings_guide.jsp
(accessed 2009). There you will also find what are called "content
descriptors," which are labels like "fantasy violence," "reference to
alcohol," "comic mischief," etc., as well as game reviews and purchasing locations, both online and in store. For more information
on game ratings, see "Organize a Monthly Video Game Tournament" in Chapter 3.

The type of console(s) your library has or plans to purchase will
affect the types of games and ratings that will most likely be available to you. The Wii is family friendly, and its games are generally
rated E for Everyone or T for Teen. Handhelds such as the
Nintendo DS and the PSP also have a large selection of E-rated

games. Both the PS3 and Xbox 360 have a large selection of T for Teen and M for Mature rated games. It is not unusual for libraries to circulate M-rated games (recommended for ages 17 and up) but not allow them to be played at the library's gaming events.

When considering content, you want to gain a deeper understanding of the games beyond just their ratings. To do so, read game reviews, seek patron recommendations, talk to any staff members who may be experienced gamers, and possibly even test a game yourself here and there.

The policies and procedures for selecting other types of materials your library may currently be circulating, such as graphic novels, music, and movies, can guide your decisions about game content as well. Whatever the decision, don't be discouraged and pass up opportunities to explore the content of the games in an informed way, such as playing prospective games, tying video game content to other formats or events at your library, and gathering anecdotes from fans of the game(s) themselves. Library policies do change. While the budget or other circumstances may prevent your games to be circulated, no matter what the rating, keep your pulse on trends and what your community and patrons are asking for through periodic surveys when a purchasing opportunity arises.

Catalog, Shelve, and Display the Games

How you choose to display your games goes hand in hand with how you catalog them. To make it the most accessible to patrons, I suggest you include information such as the number of players, the rating, the system requirements (especially if your library is not circulating consoles), and a description. Whether or not it's considered a CD-ROM or computer optical disc should be a part of the record, as well. Subject headings that reflect the game's content will not only help players determine if it is something they want to check out but will also help them draw connections between other materials of similar topics to borrow.

With regard to where to place the games in the library, some libraries shelve the video games in their audiovisual section, and others shelve them as part of the book collection (see Figure 2.2). Still others have a reserve-only collection and shelve the actual

▶ Figure 2.2: Circulating Video Games

games in a staff-only area. How your community feels about the video game collection can also dictate where it is placed. Other factors include whether you have a high rate of theft or whether the collection is targeted to a particular age group.

This is also where knowledge of the content of a video game comes in handy. While having a display of just video games is one thing and completely fine—especially to advertise gaming programs such as National Gaming Day (November) or the fact that your library circulates games—it's also great to make the connection that it's just another format to tell a story by displaying them with other materials. It would be perfectly appropriate to include physically active games such as *Mario & Sonic at the Olympics* (Sega) or *Wii Fit* (Nintendo) with other health-related materials. Games such as *Wii Music* (Nintendo) and *Donkey Konga* (Nintendo) will make a great fit alongside books about music, magazines, and audiobooks. In other words, the possibilities are pretty endless for pairing up video games with topics for display. "Gamers Are Readers: Capitalize on the Popularity of Video Games" (Eastwood and Wesson, www.schoollibraryjournal.com/article/CA6647714.html, accessed 2009), the article mentioned earlier, goes in depth about the relationship between the contents of video games and books. Developing and maintaining a circulating video collection is no easy task. If done efficiently and with your community's involvement, the positive results on the rest of the collection and attendance at programs will definitely be worth the effort and funding required for implementing such a service.

▶ CREATE PROGRAM FORMS

The following sample forms and policies can be adapted for your specific program needs:

1. Gaming Equipment Circulation (Library to Library) Form
2. Game Agreement Form
3. Gaming Unit (Nintendo DS Lite) Circulation Policy
4. Gaming Unit (Nintendo DS Lite) Borrower Responsibility Agreement
5. Gaming Equipment (GPS Units) Circulation Policy

▶ Figure 2.3: Gaming Equipment Circulation Form

[Date]		
Sent from [staff/branch name]:		[Branch name] Received:
DS Lite 2 and stylus	—	—
DS Lite 3 and stylus	—	—
4 and stylus	—	—
5 and stylus	—	—
6 and stylus	—	—
7 and stylus	—	—
8 and stylus	—	—
6 copies of *Mario Kart* cartridge	—	—
5 *Mario Kart* cases	—	—
5 *Mario Kart* booklets	—	—
2 *Zelda* cartridges	—	—
2 *Zelda* booklets	—	—
1 *Brain Age* case, booklet, and cartridge	—	—
6 power cords	—	—

▶ **Figure 2.4: Game Agreement Form**

The "After School Gaming Club" [or other name of event] is a 2-hour program for youth [ages]. The program is designed to allow like-minded youth the chance to meet in a safe location [name of library] and play video games with one another. All games will be rated "T for Teen" or "E for Everyone."

Library staff will be present throughout the entire program.

The event is scheduled from 4:00 p.m. to 6:00 p.m. on the following dates:
Tuesday, September 8
Tuesday, October 13
Tuesday, November 10

I give my child permission to bring his/her own personal *video games* to the library for the After School Gaming Club.

Name of patron: _____

Parent/Guardian signature: _____

▶ **Figure 2.5: Gaming Unit (Nintendo DS Lite) Circulation Policy**

[Name of Department/Library]

What's needed to borrow a DS Lite from [name of library]?
- It is free to check out a DS Lite if you have a valid library card (not a guest card) on file with the [name of library]. The card must be present and belong to the borrower presenting it.
- Borrower must be between the ages of 10 and 18. Borrowers ages 10 and 11 must have a parent's signature as well as their own.
- Borrower must be in good standing with the library. This means the borrower cannot owe more than $10 in charges.

Loan period
- Maximum loan period for a DS Lite is 2 hours, 1 hour if there is a waiting list.
- Failure to return the DS Lite on time or to not sign it back in may result in a block on your record resulting in a loss of borrowing or Internet privileges.
- Staff will go over the checklist (see back page) with the borrower and sign the DS Lite back in upon return of the unit.

Returns
- DS Lites must be returned and signed back in to the service desk where you checked it out at least 15 minutes prior to closing.
- The borrower agrees to return DS Lite and game(s).

Penalties
- The first time you return a DS Lite late or do not sign the DS Lite back in, you will receive a verbal warning and a note on your library card record.

(continued)

(continued)

- The second time you return a DS Lite late or do not sign the DS Lite back in, you will receive a second (and final) warning with a note on your library card record.
- The third time you return a DS Lite late or do not sign the DS Lite in you will have a block put on your record so you are unable to borrow a DS Lite for one year.

Security

- A borrowed DS Lite should never be left unattended.
- The borrower who checks out the DS Lite is ultimately responsible for it. This is nontransferable. The cost resulting from damage to or theft of a DS Lite, peripherals, and/or games will be charged to the library card account of the user.
- [Name of library] is not responsible for loss while DS Lite is checked out to a borrower.
- [Name of library] is not responsible for damage or theft of personal games that occurs while using the library's DS Lite.

The fine print

- Only one DS Lite per person may be checked out during any given time.
- Only one game per unit at a time may be checked out. Please ask staff to switch out games.
- Personal games may be used with the library's DS Lite.
- You may check out a game to use on your personal DS Lite.
- DS Lites are checked out for in-[department name] use ONLY. This means you cannot leave the [department name] area of the building with a DS Lite, even if you have it checked out. Law enforcement officers will be notified if a DS Lite is removed from [library name].
- DS Lites are to be used ONLY by the individual who has checked it out; do not lend the unit to anyone else.
- You must be ages 12–18 to play "T for Teen" rated games.

I understand and agree to abide by all policies listed above. By signing this form I am acknowledging that I am between 10 and 18 years of age and that I am in good standing with [name of library]. This signed agreement will be kept on file for 30 days from the date signed.

Print Name: _____

Signature: _____

Date: _____

Parent/Guardian Signature (10–11 year olds only):

▶ Figure 2.6: Gaming Unit (Nintendo DS Lite) Borrower Responsibility Agreement

[Name of Department/Library]

I agree to return the DS Lite unit and games in the same order and condition as when I received them and if such equipment is damaged or lost while on loan, I agree to reimburse the library for the cost of the unit and/or games.

OUT:

For Staff Use Only

Borrower Library Card Number: _____

DS Lite ID: _____

Date: _____

Staff Initials: _____

Time Out: _____

Checklist

_____ DS Lite

_____ Power Supply

_____ Game Cartridge

IN:

Checklist

_____ DS Lite

_____ Power Supply

_____ Game Cartridge

Date/Time Returned: _____/_____

*Borrower Signature: _____

Staff Initials: _____

▶ Figure 2.7: Gaming Equipment (GPS Units) Circulation Policy

[Name of Department/Library]

The following policy is in regard to checking out GPS units to patrons.

Where can I borrow the gaming equipment?

- Branches where units can be borrowed include: [branch names].
- Units do not work indoors. Geocaching is an outdoor activity, and caches will be located around the county near the library branches mentioned above.
- The library is not responsible for accidents that may occur on the property as a result of participating in this event.

What is the loan period for the GPS units?

- The checkout period for each individual GPS unit is three days. Renewals are not allowed.

(continued)

(continued)

- Failure to return the GPS unit on time, or to not to sign the unit back in from the branch it was borrowed, will result in a block on your record resulting in a loss of borrowing or Internet privileges and $100 added (cost of the unit) to your account. If the item is returned late but is not damaged, we will waive the $100 fee.
- The program will begin in [month/year] and run through [month/year]. You may check out an available GPS unit for any three-day period during this time frame. Although you cannot renew your GPS unit, you can check out another unit for another three-day period if one is available.

Where do I return the GPS unit I borrowed?

- All GPS units must be returned and signed back in at the library branch from which you borrowed it.
- If the equipment is damaged or lost while on loan, borrower agrees to reimburse the library for the cost of the unit ($100.00).

What's needed to borrow a GPS unit?

- It's free to check out a GPS unit if you have a valid library card on file with [name of library]. The card must be present to check out a GPS unit.
- The borrower must be 12 years or older, and the library card must be in the borrower's name.
- The borrower must be in good standing with the library and not owe more than $10 in fines or fees.
- Only one GPS unit may be checked out to any one library card at any given time.

What is expected in terms of the security of the GPS unit?

- A borrowed GPS unit should not be left unattended.
- Any borrower who checks out a GPS unit is ultimately responsible for the safe return of the unit to the library.
- By signing this form, the borrower agrees not to damage the unit and to return it in the same condition as received.

I understand and agree to abide by all policies listed above. By signing this form I acknowledge that I am 12 years or older and that I am in good standing with [name of library]. This signed agreement will be kept on file for 30 days from the date signed.

Print name: _____

Signature: _____

Date: _____

Staff use:

Borrower library card number:

Time out:

GPS unit ID number:

Date:

Staff initials:

Date/Time Returned: _____

Borrower Signature: _____

Staff Initials: _____

*If borrower did not sign DS Lite back in, please remember to put a staff note on the borrower's record.

▶3

IMPLEMENTATION

▶ Organize a Monthly Video Game Tournament

▶ Plan a Board Game Event

▶ Host a *Magic: The Gathering* Tournament

▶ Organize a *Guitar Hero* Fest

▶ Integrate Gaming with an Anime Fest

▶ Begin a Circulating Game Collection

▶ ORGANIZE A MONTHLY VIDEO GAME TOURNAMENT

Identify Your Target Audience

People who enjoy playing video games, more often than not, would enjoy participating in a video game tournament. Think about it. A video game tournament is a great way for gamers to test, or even show off, their gaming skills. Video game tournaments also help bring people together who might not otherwise have an opportunity to interact with each other.

When putting together a video game tournament, the first thing you should do is determine what age level or levels you will target. While you probably base the majority of your programs on groups of similar ages, keep in mind that video game skills often can transcend the age level. You could theoretically have an 18 year old play next to a 30 year old and either of the two might easily win. It's important to be clear about what age your tournament is open to so that people don't feel the rules are being changed halfway through the registration period. Here are a few scenarios that might help get you started.

Like Ages

Whether it's kids, teens, or adults, tournaments based on like ages will bring peers together who might bond over other similar interests in between and during game play. If one of your main goals is to get similar-aged people involved with one another, this may be the route to go. Same-age groups can often be together in the library and could help spread the word about the tournament to their friends. They might be able to practice together at the library before the tournament and thus get a good sense of who their competition might be.

Ages Aligned with Game Ratings

Game ratings are discussed in more detail later but are mentioned here in case you are certain at this point what game you will be using in your tournament. Most video games are assigned age-appropriate ratings by the Entertainment Software Rating Board (ESRB) (www.esrb.org, accessed 2009). If you've decided to use *Super Smash Brothers* in your tournament, for example, don't forget to check its rating (T for Teen). Knowing this should dictate the age range for those allowed to sign up independently for the tournament and those who will need permission slips (in this example, 13 and up and under 13, respectively).

All Ages

The benefit of an all-ages event is that it can bring the family together even if some members are just cheering from the sidelines. There are tons of games rated E for Everyone that are appropriate for all ages. It's a great way for young and old or experienced and newbie to mentor each other and practice teamwork. You might want to set boundaries beforehand to establish good sportsmanship.

Whatever age group you finally decide to target, stick to it and be clear with it in your advertising. Don't feel your tournament has to be all things to all people. Even if you're the only one in the library system having a tournament at this time, chances are if the patrons voice their opinions on wanting to have one for their age group, it'll give you leverage to get it going the next time around.

Ability Level

No matter what age group your tournament targets, those seeking to participate will always have differing levels of ability, and many games offer several difficulty levels, sometimes categorized as "Easy," "Medium," and "Hard." While this doesn't mean you have to have three different tournaments to accommodate all skills, it does mean that you will need to be clear when marketing the tournament which level(s) it will be played at. This is important because if you're only going to do the "Easy" level you may lose the hard-core gamers (and vice versa), but it's better that they know that up front than be disappointed when they arrive.

An opening scene from *Dance Dance Revolution* (*DDR*) is driven by a player's feet matching the corresponding arrows on the screen. Depending on which version of *DDR* you're using, the difficulty levels are broken down into "Beginner/Light/Basic," "Standard/Trick," "Heavy/Expert/Challenging" for the Game Player mode. This breakdown might look cut and dried but not every game offers the same levels, and, even within these categories, there are a lot of different ways you can organize the competition.

One common way to address ability levels and make a *DDR* tournament fair is to have one competition with "Beginner/Medium" and a separate one for "Advanced/Expert" players. Another way is to have one person pick the song and the other pick the difficulty level, and both compete against each other. A third way is to freestyle where the tournament focus is the participants appealing to the audience with impressive moves on the dance pad that still match up correctly with the arrows.

Other popular tournament games that are similar to *DDR* in terms of being broken down into ability levels are *Guitar Hero* and *Rock Band*. Other ways to address abilities if the game isn't organized into ability modes is to choose random stages or characters.

Be open to suggestions from the players of how to make a game more fair as you're developing the rules for the tournament. They will tell you! Try not to change the rules midmonth or especially midgame unless you really erred in a decision and no one is enjoying the event. Do keep track of new suggestions and implement them when appropriate.

Choose the Game

Probably one of the most important things you will have to do for the tournament is choose the game. Because you're aiming for a monthly activity, choose one that will have some sticking power for at least several months. Give it enough time, though, to build a following and develop into an expected event before deciding to switch gears.

Recommended Titles

Rock Band

Madden

Soul Calibur

Mario Kart

Pokémon

Street Fighter

Get Input from the Players

No doubt you'll want to get suggestions from people, including the players themselves. How do you get input from the players if you're not sure who they will be? You've already defined your audience, so get their attention in the same way you do for other programs:

▶ **Ask them!** Don't be shy to ask your regulars even if you're not sure if they're gamers. They probably still have an opinion. Giving them a few choices to narrow down their ideas might help.

▶ **Advertise in their area of the library.** If there is a children /tween or teen section, put a suggestion box there that lets them know you're looking for ideas. For adults, put up a flyer to let them know this is coming and you'd like their input.

▶ **Have a few open gaming events** (these are just free play events where there is no competition) and ask the participants to decide what they would like the tournament game to be.

▶ **Get their attention online.** Facebook or MySpace are great places to solicit opinions from others.

Involve Staff and the Community

If you involve library staff in the decision, they will be more likely to help you out if you need it. While this isn't the goal of asking them their opinion, don't underestimate their involvement! You might want to schedule a few days where some games can be set up in the staff lounge. You might want to enlist the help of staff who know how to play the game to show others the ropes. When you ask them to vote, give them a handout with the game title, rating, ages you're targeting, and how the activity fits in with your library's strategic focus. Be sure to include some space for them to express any concerns they may have.

Your present resources, such as space availability and budget for the games themselves, may make it necessary for you to reach out to your community. Game stores are often happy to give their time and help organize a tournament. They can also share their advice on what makes a good competitive game and suggest some rules to include. If you have the equipment, consider partnering with a parks and recreation center. They usually have space and an audience that might be looking for something fun to do. Occasionally movie theaters might get in on the activity, and they have a large screen people would love to watch and play on. Schools can be another resource for an afterschool activity. Gaming is pretty ubiquitous so don't think any partnership idea is too silly to pursue. You never know until you try.

Understand Game Ratings

The Entertainment Software Rating Board (ESRB) assigns ratings to video games using symbols and content descriptors. The symbols consist of letters (eC, E, E10+, T, M, AO, and RP). These symbols correspond with ages. For example, eC means "Early Childhood" and identifies content that is suitable for those 3 and over. M means "Mature" and identifies content that is appropriate for those 17 and older.

The content descriptors are 30 words that are factored into a game's rating. "Language," "blood," and "violence" are some examples of descriptors. For a complete list, visit www.esrb.org/ratings/ratings_guide.jsp (accessed 2009). You can search the ESRB site for their ratings of specific games by typing in the title of the game and the platform (PC, Xbox 360, Wii, etc.) it is played on. Different versions of the game may receive different ratings.

ESRB Rating Symbols

eC = Early Childhood
Titles rated eC have content suitable for ages 3 and older. Titles will contain no material that parents would find inappropriate.

E = Everyone
Titles rated E have content suitable for ages 6 and older. Titles may contain minimal cartoon, fantasy, or mild violence and/or infrequent use of mild language.

E 10+ = Everyone 10 and older
Titles rated E10+ have content suitable for ages 10 and older. Titles in this category may contain more cartoon, fantasy, or mild violence; mild language; and/or minimal suggestive themes.

T = Teen
Titles rated T have content suitable for ages 13 and older. Titles may contain violence, suggestive themes, crude humor, minimal blood, simulated gambling, and/or infrequent use of strong language.

M = Mature
Titles rated M have content suitable for persons ages 17 and older. Titles may contain intense violence, blood and gore, sexual content, and/or strong language.

AO = Adults Only
Titles rated AO have content suitable only for persons 18 years and older. Titles may include prolonged scenes of intense violence and/or graphic sexual content and nudity.

RP = Rating Pending
Titles listed as RP have been submitted to the ESRB and are awaiting final rating. (This symbol appears only in advertising prior to a game's release.)

(ESRB Ratings, www.esrb.org/ratings/ratings_guide.jsp, accessed 2009)

Keep in mind that these ratings are guides, not strict rules, for one to follow. While many libraries across the country allow those under 17 to play games with an M rating, such as *Halo*, they often do so with written parental permission. Visit the Edwardsville (IL) Library gaming blog for examples of M-rated games that are played without requiring parental permission (http://gamingatyourlibrary.com, accessed 2009). You will know your community and how closely you should stick to the age guides. We often toe the line when it comes to purchasing controversial books or magazines for our collection. Games can sometimes require the same considerations. We may want to allow certain songs and not others in a tournament with a music-related game, for example. That's your call and a perfectly legitimate one. Just be sure to be clear before the tournament starts. You don't want participants to be practicing a certain song only to come and find out that they can't play it.

Also, before you decide to ban all fighting games for a tournament, expose yourself to research that indicates most players know the difference between playing a game with a virtual opponent versus acting out such behaviors in real life. The fact that screen play can often be a great outlet for pent-up aggression can be helpful. *Grand Theft Childhood: The Surprising Truth about Violent Video Games and What Parents Can Do* (Kutner and Olson, 2008) is a great resource for examining some of these issues. In general, it's a good idea to have a balance of all types of games for a tournament no matter what their genres are.

Set Game Parameters

Rules and Regulations

Although you won't know every facet of a game, you can't possibly establish sound tournament rules without having a basic understanding of the game you chose. Here are some steps you can take to develop good tournament rules.

Become familiar with the game. Play the game yourself, ask questions from more seasoned players, and ask someone to give you a general outline.

Order a strategy guide for your library's collection. The guide will give you an overview of the game and will give players ideas on how to improve their game play.

Check the forums boards on the Internet for your particular game, as chances are good that the game you have chosen has been played in a tournament somewhere before. The URL might be listed in the strategy guide, or do a general search on the Internet using the game title and "forum board" as key words. Within the forums boards is information on where tournaments are taking place and what rules they are using. Use them as a basis to come up with yours.

Post an e-mail inquiry or check the archives of the LibGaming Google Groups listserv (http://groups.google.com/group/ LibGaming, accessed 2009). This is an online community of over 600 members—many of whom are librarians—to share knowledge and resources about gaming with each other. A frequently posted question is, "I'm having a tournament at my library for X game. If you've ever had a tournament before for this game, what were your rules?" Also, consult *Gamers. . .in the Library?!* (Neiburger, 2009) for some more in-depth pointers on running tournaments.

Some of your rules will be based on the time you have allowed for the tournament. For example, if you are using a game such as *Rock Band* or *Guitar Hero,* where certain songs are very long, you will probably want to have a list of songs that both can and can't be in the tournament. Other games, such as *Super Smash Brothers Brawl,* can be set so that a match takes place and is over within a certain time limit.

Another rule you will want to be clear about from the get-go is how you will score the game so that it's the most fair. A *DDR* tournament, for example, can be judged a variety of ways. The winner could be determined based on the combined score at the end that flashes on the screen or on the number of Perfects/Goods/Greats (based on how close the step on the *DDR* pad was to the beat).

Your rules need to take into consideration any varying levels of play the game may have. Many games, including *DDR,* can be played on a range of levels. For example, the songs are usually slower on the easier levels. Perhaps you have the most difficult levels compete against one another, or have two tournaments, one for those who want to play at a basic level and one for those who want to play at a more difficult level. This will help keep things fair for all and give players a challenge that won't lead to frustration if they are new at the game.

Don't be afraid to change the rules for your tournament if need be. Not midgame, of course, but if it's a monthly event, then next month. Integrating a new rule recommended by the players or getting rid of one that doesn't seem to work is all part of improving the overall tournament. Keep a record of the changes, and you can be the next resource for someone inquiring how to have their own tournament!

Scoring Tools

Many tournaments will accommodate a bracket setup such as the one found at www.crowsdarts.com/brackets/tourn.html (accessed 2009). Single elimination means that players cycle through the tournament one time only. As soon as they lose, they are finished for that day. Double elimination means that if they lose one time, they still have a chance to continue and even win the entire tournament if they keep on winning. Because double elimination can be a little tricky, especially if you have a fairly large number of players, it's recommended to do a practice run-through on paper before your event so that you feel comfortable with how it works. Make up names and fill them in the slots according to the directions for your practice round. Consider using a whiteboard to make the results from the brackets visible (see Figure 3.1). Players usually are eager to know who they are playing as well as where they stand during the tournament!

Scoring software is also available online. One system was created by Ann Arbor District Library and is available at http://gtsystem .org (accessed 2009). In part, what this software does is automatically create brackets for you depending on what input you give, such as what game, how many players, etc. One of the benefits of using this online software is that you can project it on a screen and players will see their rank immediately.

Prizes

You will likely consider offering prizes for tournament winners at some point. There may be several "in house" awards, such as more computer time, fine reductions, or a free DVD rental, that you can offer that won't break your bank. If you do apply for a grant, include prizes such as gift certificates to gaming stores in your request. You can also ask for community donations or for your library's Friends group to fund prizes.

Give your local game stores a call and ask to speak to the manager about a community partnership. Let the managers know who you are, the reason for your call, and that you'd like to stop in to see if they might be able to contribute something in exchange for helping to advertise their company name. When you stop in, bring a copy of your flyers, your business card, and a letter to the appro-

▶ Figure 3.1: Visible Brackets

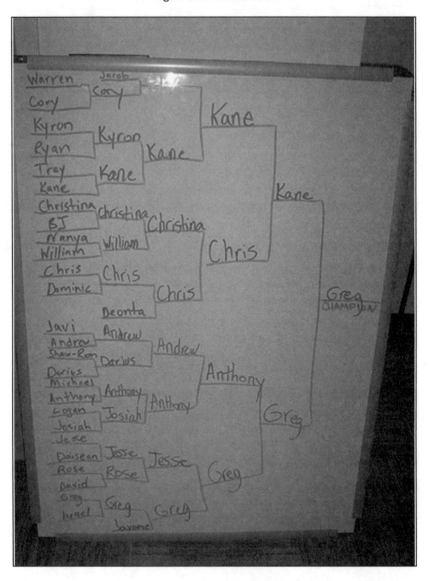

priate person (make sure you have the person's name spelled correctly!). If you've already held a few gaming events, tell them about your audience turnouts and some anecdotes that have come out of having the tournaments. Do the gamers typically use the library for more than just the gaming programs? Chances are a game store will love to support a more literate community! Finally, an incentive for café-type game stores (where people can play video games by the hour) to contribute to your tournament is that you'll probably bring them more customers.

Prepare for the Game

Plan for the Cost

While it's usually fine to ask participants to bring their own equipment, you will likely want to purchase some equipment if you're preparing for a monthly event. Putting effort into advertising for an event where the equipment may or may not be present probably won't sit well with the gamers! You will also want to set aside funding for replacement accessories. Controllers and other peripherals can get broken from repeated use or misplaced fairly easily. **You do not need to invest in brand new equipment**, particularly if you don't have the funding. Most game stores sell refurbished games, consoles, and peripherals at a cheaper rate.

It's good to do a mock setup of everything you think you will need for your tournament so that you can add anything to your shopping list that you might not have anticipated, such as an extension cord, power strip, or a wireless (versus wired) sensor bar for Wii games or wireless/wired guitar for *Guitar Hero*. If you want multiple screens to accommodate additional players, consider investing in used television sets. Most games require sound, so you'll want to make sure you have a good set of speakers, other than the ones included with your projector, that will allow for optimum surround sound effect. Remember, you can always add to your equipment trove. If you have a screen that is really old but is still fine to use for game play, roll with it until the next budget cycle comes around.

Determine the Duration of the Game

Keep in mind the length of each round when determining the duration of each game in the tournament. If you only have exactly two hours for an event, then calculate how many rounds can fit in that amount of time. You will want to limit some games to a certain length so they don't go on for what seems like forever. For *Super Smash Brothers*, for example, a three-minute time limit is generally a good amount for each round. For *Madden*, a five-minute quarter is a suggested time and a limit on the point differential between the players before the game is called. Otherwise, frequent passing stops the clock and can slow down the game. If you're not sure where to start when developing your game rules, ask the avid players for their advice.

Decide When the Event Should Take Place

You will know your library best in terms of how much flexibility you have in scheduling programs. You may be restricted to having such an event only during certain times or days of the week. However, if the calendar is more wide open, you should consider a few things. If the noise level will be an issue, involve a few staff to see when might be a good time for both you and your audience to have such an event. Be aware of any large community events, such as a day off school, that might increase or decrease your audience numbers, again depending on who it is you want to reach. Don't discount asking some of your regulars for their suggestions.

Identify Space Needs

Choose an appropriately sized place for your tournament. Know the capacity of the room so that you're not breaking the fire code. Use a hand counter to tally the number of people entering so that you know when you've reached capacity. Require registration of players beforehand and clearly advertise the total number of participants that can play so all participants understand and none are disappointed. If possible, reserve the room at least a half hour before the program and a half hour after to set up and clean up.

It's also highly recommended to do a run-through of your event at least a week in advance. Make sure all of your outlets work by plugging in the cords you will use. If they don't work, rearrange your setup or purchase an extension cord to use with an outlet that does work. Are the cords in the way of traffic flow more than you anticipated? Use some kind of barrier, such as chairs or stanchions, to block off any potential tripping hazards. Duct tape will do the job but can leave sticky residue on your extension cords over time. A long-term solution may be smooth plastic covers that just lay on top of the cords. If you notice anything in the room, such as excess furniture that would be helpful if moved out during your event, check if that can be done. If not and you're able to place barriers such as tables in front, by all means, do so. You want to be able to concentrate on the game play and have a good time—not worry.

Some games, such as *DDR, Guitar Hero,* and *Rock Band,* are inherently noisy because they involve music. Others, such as *Madden* and *NBA Live,* may be loud because they involve spectator sports. While it's always within your purview to limit the number of players in the tournament, it is also good to keep in mind limiting spectators. After-hours tournaments may be the best option for the excessive noise levels or if you don't have an enclosed room for game play. Posting advance notices of noise a week or so ahead of time may be enough to give patrons the heads-up that things may be louder than usual for a few hours. Forming partnerships within the community such as recreation centers can come in handy when noise can become an issue.

Get Staff and Volunteers to Assist

If you have another staff member available to help, even if it's just for when the event starts or ends, you will be glad you did. You can always ask a trusted participant if they'd be willing to lend a hand if you're short staffed. Here are some things they can help you with:

- ▶ Checking people in and putting their names into brackets (if that's how you organize your tournament). Include in your publicity when you expect people at the event and when registration cuts off. Many people may wander in an hour after the game started. They cannot be added into a bracket at that point and may be unexpectedly disappointed. Remind them they can always stay and cheer people on!
- ▶ Taking photographs or videotaping your event. Be familiar with your library's policy regarding taking images at library events. You may need to include permission information as part of your advertising or be prepared at the door with permission slips. If someone wishes not to be photographed, make sure your volunteer photographer knows it!
- ▶ Emceeing to keep the energy level up and to give play-by-play commentary. You will need a microphone with speakers, depending on the size of your room and the noise level allowed. This equipment is something you will want to test out in the room with a lot of people. You also might want to audition a few

people before your event to see if they are an appropriate fit for the job. Being familiar with the game if they are going to be commentators will help!

▶ Providing crowd control. For the most part, the participants are there because they want to be there and don't want to make behavioral decisions that will ruin it for everyone else. However, you know your library community the best. If your library provides security guards, be familiar with the procedure to request their presence at your event.

You should alert staff and volunteers at least several weeks if not months beforehand so they can adjust their schedules. Because you probably won't be able to leave the room for long (or even short) periods of time, you'll want someone else present. If you do not have extra staff or security, consider having a two-way radio to communicate with the staff at the reference desk. It is also important to notify the reference staff about your event so they are aware of what is going on. Sometimes, the number of tournament participants will be limited solely by how many staff members you can find to commit to the event. If you have a sudden cancellation of security or extra staff, adjust the amount of people allowed in the room accordingly.

Give all players a brief overview of behavioral expectations before play commences. Have an extra screen or console or a few board games available. When people have something to do, they will find less ways to get themselves into trouble. Even displays highlighting programming information or materials will give people something to do while waiting.

Keep Equipment Secure

Orange, cheese-covered fingers and gaming controllers isn't a good mix. If you're serving food during the event, be clear about the rules concerning food. Signage, placement of the food away from the gaming equipment, and a verbal reiteration can help with this. Have hand wipes and garbage cans available. Consider serving water instead of sticky, sugary drinks like soda. Keeping the water at room temperature is recommended to cut down on finding half-consumed bottles all over the room after the event.

▶ PLAN A BOARD GAME EVENT

Identify Your Target Audience

It is safe to say that most libraries carry board games. It is also likely that most of your patrons have had some experience in board game open play. A library will typically have a variety of board games available for different ages with no organized program around their use other than to just sit down and play. This kind of activity pairs well with other simultaneous events, as board games can be quite self-guided.

The open play experience has probably given you an idea of which games are most popular at your library. From watching what your patrons are playing, you can begin to formulate a plan for your board game tournament. By choosing a game that is popular, you will ensure a high level of interest in the tournament, which can lead to higher levels of socialization, participation, learning, and fun. The audience for your board game tournament is also an important determining factor to which type of game you choose, as the tournament will be a great opportunity to align with one of the library's outreach goals. For example, if your library wants to do a more targeted outreach toward ESL learners, or provide more intergenerational programming, or even improve literacy development for middle-schoolers, a board game tournament may be the perfect fit.

Sometimes gender is something to consider when setting up a board game tournament. Libraries will target programs to a specific gender in order to get more participation. For example, if you're looking to get more females involved, you could contact clubs such as the Girl Scouts or advertise the event as a "Mom's Night Out." Again, open play events are a good yardstick with which to measure the response for a potential tournament game (e.g., do more males or females gravitate toward the Scrabble board?).

If your library is brand new to board gaming, then you may need to take another route to identify your target audience. This shouldn't be hard as the activity of board gaming is so fluid as to engage a wide range of ages. Keep in mind that whatever age group you do decide to target, you still have options to engage other age groups with a few self-guided activities, which will be explored later in this section.

Determine Level of Play

Of course everyone who will want to be in the tournament will not have the same ability or experience level. While a tournament usually brings players together who aren't completely new to the game, consider offering a few open play or practice sessions a few weeks beforehand to give people the opportunity to pick up some tips and tricks to improve their game play before the tournament. If players are asking for a more intense tournament with experienced players, consider having the option for participants to self-select what level they want to participate in (beginner, moderate, or advanced). Provide brief explanations of what each of those levels mean, such as if they have played for a certain number of years, typically score within a range of points, or are part of a club that regularly plays that particular game.

Age is a good determining factor for the level of play for a tournament. You will probably want to choose an age for eligibility that is no less than a specified number meant for the game to be played in the tournament. For example, a Monopoly game tournament is typically recommended to be for those no younger than eight years of age.

Choose the Game

Scott Nicholson, Professor of Library Science at Syracuse University and Chief Scientist of the Library Game Lab, suggests that "if libraries want to have a board game tournament, then a mainstream game is the way to go. One reason is since people are generally expected to be well-practiced, sticking with the games that most people will find familiar will bring in a higher turnout" (e-mail interview, November 2009). For suggestions on a variety of board games via a short video episode, visit Board Games with Scott (www.boardgameswithscott.com, accessed 2009).

Mainstream board games for a tournament include Scrabble, Monopoly, Yahtzee, Chess, Sorry!, Trouble, Checkers, and Dungeons & Dragons (D&D). You will know your community best and what game they might be asking for to participate in as a tournament experience. Because you have already chosen your target audience based on age, ability level, or gender, match those with your game.

Keep in mind that there are different versions of a game that might fit one age group better than another. For example, there is Scrabble and Scrabble Junior or Monopoly and Monopoly Junior.

The number of players the game will allow (Checkers and Chess allow two, other games such as Sorry! and Trouble allow up to four) can also help you decide which game to pick. Even though a game may allow "up to" a certain number of players, you can establish a rule for the maximum number of players per copy of the game. If you want a game that is for only two players, you will definitely need multiple copies. If it's an eight-player game such as Monopoly, having a few copies would be helpful but theoretically could be done with one or two copies and allowing up to eight players each if you're aiming for a smaller tournament experience.

Library Logistics Affect the Game You Choose

Sometimes the logistics of your library will be a determining factor to which game you choose. If you don't have a space available for more than two hours, a Monopoly tournament for the serious gamer is not going to work. You would want at least half a day or partner with a community organization to use their space for a long stretch of time. You can always modify the game play to accommodate library time and space restrictions and limit game play in hour segments and have a very successful event, but, if you want to attract the serious gamers from time to time, you'll want to have some options for flexibility.

The amount of time your space is available will also be a factor in deciding whether to have a qualifying or preliminary round for the game and then a final. Seating players, explaining the rules and expectations, and announcing the winners are all some of the other activities that will take time too and you'll need to plan for when reserving the room and organizing your time.

Noise is also a consideration when planning a space for the tournament. You want the players to be able to socialize but also to have a bit of a quiet space so that they can concentrate on their game play. If this isn't possible to arrange in the space available at your library, opt to try to schedule it at a low-traffic time or partner with a local organization that might be able to better accommodate for a quiet yet social experience.

Set Game Parameters

Rules and Regulations

If you're taking part in an "official" tournament, you of course need to abide by the rules of the sponsoring organization. Registration and advertising within their guidelines are some of the areas that a typical official tournament requires. Because most libraries are unable to charge for events unless it's a specific fundraising activity, you'll want to make sure to find out if admission or entry fees are required and your library's policy before signing on to host such an event.

Audience Input

You probably sought input from your patrons when deciding what game to use for the tournament. Don't be afraid to ask their help again to modify the game rules to accommodate your time constraints, number of board games, or any other limitations you might have. Players will be happy to give their opinions to help make it a fair and enjoyable experience for all. If possible, have some open play events in the weeks before your tournament to work out any game play rules that might come up that you hadn't thought about.

If you're aiming for a more intense experience for players with a game you're not an expert at, consider contacting a local board game store and see if they would be willing to help out.

Prizes

Gift certificates to local stores, movie passes, fine waivers, dinner coupons, massage coupons for adults, or something tied into the time of year your tournament is held, such as "back to school" supplies or Halloween candy, all make for good prizes. Again, get input from your patrons as you're developing the tournament. Ask them what might motivate them to participate. If your budget doesn't allow for the cost of prizes, asking for donations is acceptable. Offer to include the donor business or organization's logo on your advertising.

If you have neither donations nor budget for prizes, "fame" is always a good compromise. Post the winners (in compliance with your library's privacy policy) on your Web site or capture some footage of the game play and upload it so that stellar moves—particularly the winning one—can be viewed over and over again. Just make sure you're transparent about what the prize will be in your advertising, as it will probably be a frequently asked question.

Prepare for the Game

Plan for the Cost

Most mainstream board games cost from $5.00 to $20.00 per game. After the holidays can be a great time to get a bargain. If you have an ideal number of copies in mind you would like, but don't have the funds, chances are someone who works at the library will own one and be able to lend it for the event. If you're looking to have a more sustainable collection and be able to have funds for replacement costs, stores such as Walmart, Target, and Best Buy are some avenues to consider. Funagain Games (www .funagain.com, accessed 2009) gives monthly grants to educators, including libraries, for board and card games.

> For a list of other suggested granting organizations, visit the ALA Gaming Toolkit at http:// librarygamingtoolkit.org/grants .html.

Identify Space Needs

Most board game tournaments take place with multiple copies of the same game in the same space, spread out over several tables, running simultaneously. Here is a short list of things to consider when organizing the physical setup for your board game tournament:

> ▶ Make sure the tables are set up to allow ample space for players to get up and move around. You do not want people crammed into such close proximity that might interfere with game play. "Too close for comfort" could also be a security issue by causing already high tensions to escalate.

▶ The number of chairs at the table should match the number of possible players and a judge if you plan to have one. Onlookers can watch from the sidelines if your room allows it, but no need to add a bunch of extra chairs to one table if it's only a four-person game.

▶ Make sure the area is well ventilated.

▶ If the tournament will take place outside, have a backup plan for bad weather, including wind that can blow the equipment around.

▶ Allocate space for wheelchairs or other mobile equipment people might be using, such as crutches or walkers. Be mindful of those who may need to be near the door for easy exit.

▶ Be aware of the room capacity to comply with the fire code.

▶ Keep a balance of space for players and viewers if your room allows. You may want to include in the program description whether or not nontournament players can be present. You will also want room for players who are eliminated from the tournament, if possible.

A practice setup of the room before the actual day of the tournament is one way to prepare for any unintended issues. Having a staff member do a walk-through of your setup to provide a second pair of eyes is another way to get ready for a successful event.

Get Staff and Volunteers to Assist

You should have at least two helpers available during the tournament. Inviting a volunteer to help with some of the tasks can be a great way for people to connect with the library. You may also have some staff members who are particularly interested in games. If your event is geared toward the more serious gamers, you may want to consider volunteer judges. At least one judge per eight players is recommended. There are a number of ways your helpers can assist:

▶ Checking people in when they arrive (announcing when the start time will be as part of your advertising and setting a cutoff date and time for registration will help the tournament commence on time)

▶ Explaining the tournament rules and library/organization expectations when all are assembled

▶ Leaving the room to retrieve materials if something is forgotten or needs to be replaced

▶ Judging for game play disputes (must be familiar with the game for this job!)

▶ Being game scorekeepers or timekeepers

▶ Taking pictures or shooting video

▶ Monitoring the security of the equipment

▶ Assisting other patrons if the tournament is in close proximity to other activities taking place

▶ Monitoring crowd behavior

▶ Being prepared for the unexpected!

If it's not possible to have at least two helpers at the event for the entire time, make modifications. Perhaps you don't serve food in the same room (or serve food period) to cut down on having less to monitor in terms of spills and Cheetos-covered pieces.

If the unexpected happens and a scheduled staff member or volunteer cancels at the last minute, make sure you have a two-way radio in the room to communicate with other staff. Tell the players you're a little shorthanded and you would appreciate their help with checking people in or judging disputes. Be comfortable with a basic understanding of the game rules and game play so you're not completely lost!

Have Other Activities in the Room

More people than just those who participate in the tournament will attend the event, so it's common to have other board games available for open play in the same area where the tournament is taking place. These people will include those who arrived too late to sign up but still want to be part of the fun, siblings who got dropped off with their older brother or sister who's in the tournament, and some who were eliminated early and need something to occupy their time. Whatever the reason, if you have the space and the extra games, consider making it an informal part of the tournament.

Create displays of materials that can be checked out for people to browse. They don't have to be focused on board games. Displays can feature the newest arrivals that match the targeted age group for the tournament or materials from other community organizations. The local board game store might not be able to help run your tournament, but you can still promote their events in a display. Advertising library events such as summer reading with flyers or just by word of mouth are appropriate to include as well.

Address Food Issues

You'll need to decide whether or not to have food during your event. Based on your library's policy, food might need to be in another area apart from the tournament itself. If you're having the event at another organization, be familiar with their food policy as well. If you are having a tournament for half a day, you'll probably want to at least have water on hand, even if it's the small plastic bottles. If you're having a shorter event but don't want the attendees to fill up right before game play, serve the food afterward as part of the celebration.

▶ HOST A *MAGIC: THE GATHERING* TOURNAMENT

Magic: The Gathering (*MTG*) is a collectible card game published by Wizards of the Coast (www.wizards.com, accessed 2009). The basis of the card game is a battle between powerful wizards who use magic (dictated by the cards) to try to defeat their opponents. For a complete history, explanation of the game and how it is played, and rules, visit the *Magic: The Gathering* Wikipedia site at: http://en .wikipedia.org/wiki/Magic:_The_Gathering (accessed 2009).

If this is your first experience with *MTG*, it's recommended that you play before you are a judge. This will acclimate you to the different strategies used in tournament play and familiarize you with how the rules are leveraged in actual play. You will also be able to recognize someone who is cheating. In fact, playing a few practice games beforehand will help ensure that all the players have a good time! "Learn to Play" videos are located on the Web site of Wizards of the Coast (www.wizards.com/Magic/TCG/Article.aspx?x= mtg/tcg/newtomagic/learntoplay, accessed 2009). They are approximately one to six minutes long.

MTG fits in well with reading and literacy themes because it is linked to a paperback series (www.wizards.com/magic/novels/ magicnovels.aspx, accessed 2009). Struggling readers may start by reading the cards and then be introduced to the series as they get more comfortable in their skills and recognize the characters from the cards and game play. If running an *MTG* tournament at the library on a fairly regular basis, you will likely bring in additional foot traffic and perhaps reach segments of your population you weren't serving as much before.

Identify Your Target Audience

MTG tournaments are popular in schools, universities, bars, and gaming stores, and the game can accommodate a wide range of skill levels and ages (generally everyone over age ten, as anyone younger might have too much trouble grasping the fundamentals necessary to play). A target audience of male preteens through college age would fit like a glove. Girls and women do play and enjoy *MTG*, but their numbers are not as strong. You can expect regular readers of fantasy and science fiction to participate, so display selected fantasy and science fiction books near the tournament site.

It's a good idea to poll players to ensure that you hold the tournament at a time and date that's convenient for them. Avoid things like movie openings, sporting events, and other recreational endeavors that would be likely to compete with your target audience if at all possible.

Choose the Game

Variations of *Magic*

Be sure to read the rules (www.wizards.com/Magic/TCG/Article.aspx?x=magic/rules, accessed 2009) before organizing a tournament. Read them well in advance of the tournament, because they're extensive. You will want a copy of the rules on hand or have a computer nearby that will let you look up a given rule if you get lost. Be familiar with the DCI (www.wizards.com/Default.asp?x=dci/welcome, accessed 2009), which is the organization that determines the rules and tournament procedures for *MTG* play.

One variation is called a "draft tournament." If you choose this variation, first, of course, make sure that you know the DCI rules so that it's official. You will also need to involve the library's Friends group or have some means of funding available, because there is a nominal registration fee required. At the start of a draft tournament, players are given a set number of booster packs to open right then and there. Players have to play with what was given them, i.e., the cards in the booster packs. While in some ways this is a much harder tournament for most players, the draw is the challenge of playing with cards received by luck.

There are two types of organized play, "constructed" and "limited." In a constructed event, players arrive with their own 60-card decks (or each player is given one if you are providing) and can have no more than four copies of a named card except for "basic lands" cards. They can have a 15-card sideboard or no sideboard. The sideboard can be used to replace cards in the deck after each game. Within a constructed event there are variations in tournament formats that dictate which card sets can and can't be used and which cards within the sets are allowed or not for game play.

Limited tournaments are played with a pool of at least 40 cards. The sideboard is in effect with any left over cards, and there can be more than four copies of a named card, unlike in organized play. Booster packs are given to players in variations of a limited tournament. Six booster packs for a "sealed deck" tournament and three per player (usually there are eight players total) for a "booster draft" tournament.

You will want to draw up brackets for your tournament. You must have at least ten players for a tournament event. The Web site www.printyourbrackets.com (accessed 2009) will let you easily input the number of players. It's a good idea to enlarge a copy of the brackets or project it on a screen so that participants can see how far they have progressed and easily refer to it.

As mentioned earlier, brackets can also be done online with the GT System software (http://gtsystem.org, accessed 2009) created by the Ann Arbor District Library. You input the name of the game you are playing (because they don't have every single game possible listed, you would choose the card game Pokémon and it would set up your brackets the same as using paper for *MTG*) and the number of people, and brackets are created. Self-registration can be enabled. The winners and losers are automatically put in brackets once you tell the computer who won or lost that round. In other words, the online software is very efficient and does a lot of the work for you. Because it's online, the computer screen can easily be projected and everyone can follow their progress.

The GT System is more than just an isolated bracket for your tournament. It includes the option for preregistration to have player logos and leader boards uploaded, allowing players to feel like they are an important part of the online community at large. It also provides the opportunity for event promotion. For more information on how to use the GT System software, visit www.wiki .gtsystem.org (accessed 2009).

Set Game Parameters

Prizes

Involve your audience before the event to get their opinion on what they think would make good prizes. Booster packs are a great inexpensive gift. If you want to be considered the coolest library on the block, you might consider offering a box of boosters as the prize. Contact Wizards of the Coast (www.wizards.com, accessed 2009) to see if they have any freebies or giveaways. Library prizes such as fine reductions or free DVD rentals for the latest releases are also sure to be a hit. Gift cards for iTunes or the local gaming store will probably interest your players, as well.

Prepare for the Game

Cost of Your Tournament

MTG is an inexpensive hobby, as core packs (249 cards) and tournament packs are under $20.00 and booster packs (15 cards) are under $5.00. Players will need to get 60 cards to have a functional deck or 40 for a draft tournament. Each player will need a deck to play a game of *Magic*, so plan accordingly when organizing the tournament. Involving players in helping you decide how many packs to purchase given the budget that you have is a great idea. If your library has absolutely no budget to spring for cards, it is completely acceptable to just provide the space and ask participants to bring their own. Wizards of the Coast have provided libraries with free materials to run a tournament in the past. It's recommended to contact them to see what they might be able to offer. Used cards can also be purchased from eBay (www.ebay.com, accessed 2009) or yard sales.

Online play is possible too but with a fee that is mostly equivalent to the paper version. An online player would still need to purchase a physical deck to play offline and vice versa.

Typical Duration of Game Play

MTG is so appealing because it's scalable. It can be played by two or more players at a time. Players can also form teams with one another or play with no one on their team. Games of seven to eight people can take about four hours to play if everyone is of equal skill. For tournaments, you will need at least ten people.

Noise of Game and Players

Players state their moves as they cast, and an opponent has an opportunity to counterspell an attack. Sometimes the back and forth can be heated, so playing in a quiet portion of the library is not recommended. *MTG* is a little more vocal than Chess and in general less vocal and noisy than platform gaming. A small study room or out-of-the-way nook should suffice in curbing volume issues for casual play.

Equipment

Card or folding tables, folding chairs, and a projector or poster for bracketing are necessary items for tournament play. If you are taking registration, make sure the numbers of tables and chairs match the number who have signed up!

Space Needs

Make sure the room is well ventilated and that there are a few chairs for those who are just watching the tournament or who pass by the room and want to see what's going on. If you are providing food, a table with water and chips or granola bars nearby should be sufficient. Structuring a specific time when eating will be allowed might help with traffic and messes. *MTG* events can get quite large at the regional level, so it might be a good idea for the library to set a registration limit if it appears that demand for the game is outpacing the facilities on hand. For example, a good 30–40 people typically might be able to cram in at the local game store for a tournament. About 20 would play at any given time while the rest wandered about or walked to a nearby restaurant.

As a library with limited space, you may want to set some boundaries, such as people need to be in the tournament in order to eat the food. Otherwise, you might have many people wandering in just to eat and end up filling up the space over capacity. It would be helpful to have a staff member at the door to keep an eye on the crowd level.

Safety and Security

Players should be advised that their decks are their responsibility. If players have a deck or two, they should be able to simply keep them in their pockets in order to avoid theft. Owners should be within reach of their binders if they are trading cards. Particularly valuable cards should be left at home.

If you have extra staff on hand to help, you'll probably want to plan for two or three—in addition to the crowd monitor—to help run a tournament. One would keep track of bracketing and progression of the game, one could settle or diffuse any disputes that might occur, and another could help with prizes or directional questions that might arise during play. One judge who's used to handling a tournament is sufficient, but it's ideal to have two or three people on hand because this large of a group can be a bit daunting for the uninitiated.

Food

Light snacks such as chips or granola bars and water are appropriate food choices. Involving the players in deciding what to offer or even asking them to donate a dollar if they want refreshments might help ensure some follow-through with cleanup afterward. It's recommended to have a structured time to eat, either before the event or during a break in the middle, so as not to handle the cards with sticky fingers. Keeping hand sanitizer on hand or plenty of paper towels will help give your gaming materials more longevity.

Other Activities in the Room

Because not all participants will move up in the ranks, and some could be eliminated early, it's a good idea to have an array of leisure materials to keep the interest of idle players. Showcasing your library's role-playing, science fiction, and fantasy collections during the tournament will probably result in a circulation boost. A video game on the side for folks who have been eliminated will probably be a sure hit as well.

The section on *Magic:*
***The Gathering* was written by BWS Johnson:**

Dreadfully dejected after not finding a horde of gold after much questing about, BWS Johnson turned curmudgeon and now dwells in the hamlet of Arlington in the shire of Virginia. The University of Illinois in Urbana–Champaign forgot their rights to a mulligan, and as a result was forced to award a Master's in Library Science to the wiley Johnson, some years back.

▶ ORGANIZE A *GUITAR HERO* FEST

Guitar Hero is a very popular video game. Its controllers resemble musical instruments, allowing players to "play music" by pressing the appropriate key as it scrolls across the screen (see Figure 3.2). In 2008, Activision, the distributors of *Guitar Hero*, reported $1 billion for the franchise retail sales in North America—not including song download revenue (www.edge-online.com/news/guitar-hero -breaks-1-bln, accessed 2009).

One of the reasons for *Guitar Hero*'s success is its popularity among both male and female gamers. *Guitar Hero* has many similarities to and crossovers with older games like Konami's *DDR* and *Karaoke Revolution*, which have proven to have a strong female fan base. A recent Nielsen report maintains that *Guitar Hero* for the Wii has "engaged an older female gamer like never before" (http:// blog.nielsen.com/nielsenwire/consumer/every-gaming-system-has -its-fans-but-women-like-wii, accessed 2009). Because *Guitar Hero* can be played on almost every console (including the mobile phone), more and more consoles are seeing increased usage from both genders.

▶ Figure 3.2: *Guitar Hero* Guitars

With digital music and services such as iTunes and the iPod becoming increasingly popular, it's no wonder *Guitar Hero* is capturing the interest of the mass market. Popular shows such as *American Idol*, which has a digital interactive component of accepting votes via text, have also fueled the fire for forms of music that require digital involvement.

Identify Your Target Audience

Because all of the games in the *Guitar Hero* franchise so far are rated T by the ESRB (Teen ages 13 and up), depending on your library's policies and how comfortable the administrators are regarding the lyrics, players are recommended to be at least 13 years old. If younger players are clamoring for a music tournament of their own, there is no shortage of games such as *Donkey Konga* and *Wii Music* that are rated appropriate for younger ages to play. Songs from the 1960s and 1970s are not uncommon in the *Guitar Hero* games, which might be a way to bring in older adults who were teenagers when Fleetwood Mac's "Go Your Own Way" was popular.

Songs on the playlist are organized by difficulty levels. The less notes in the songs and the less keys on the guitar to play generally are the criteria for putting a song in the easiest level versus a higher difficulty level where the song has more notes and a more difficult combination of notes to play. Typically *Guitar Hero* tournaments will place together players who are in a similar difficulty level. In other words, a player at the "Easy" level would not be paired against someone playing on "Expert," as it wouldn't be fun or fair for anyone involved. While scores are weighted by the game itself to allow for more fairness, competitive energy for a tournament is more in sync if players from similar levels are paired. Generally, players self-select their level, and the tournament publicity includes what level(s) will be allowed for the event and how that will be organized.

If a library has more than one *Guitar Hero* set, it may want to run a simultaneous tournament with Easy and Medium levels competing against each other and Hard and Expert competing with the other set. If you know any *Guitar Hero* players at your library, get their input on how to organize the event.

Like most video games, *Guitar Hero* is likely to draw in an audience of onlookers. While your players may be a majority of one gender over another, the viewers will likely be a mixture of both and eager to watch and cheer for their favorite players.

Choose the Game

Versions of *Guitar Hero*

Five major versions of *Guitar Hero* exist. The game was first published in 2005 by RedOctane, and it has since grown to *Guitar Hero World Tour,* which came out in 2008 and allows for a four-person band to include vocals and drums (similar to MTV Games' *Rock Band* gaming series), and *Guitar Hero 5,* which came out in early fall 2009.

Let's take a brief look at some of the major differences of each version. While it's best to run a tournament with the most recent version, you may be limited by funds or your core group of gamers may advocate for one version over another. I recommend that you get patron input (as well as their reasoning for their recommendations) if you do have the funding to purchase the version of *Guitar Hero* they suggest. Chances are they will give helpful insight about the difficulty levels that you can balance against what audience you're really trying to target for the tournament. This is the time also to consider funding for downloading additional songs for the game down the road (and can be purchased with "in game" cash based on completing songs successfully at higher difficulty levels), which will keep the game fresh for players.

▶ *Guitar Hero 2* (2006) (PS2 and Xbox 360). This version has individual difficulty levels so that two players can rock simultaneously at their preferred level. Its practice mode is helpful for improving play as well as to giving newer players the chance to perfect their skills, especially when trying out their fingers on the "Hard" level. It allows for online play with the Xbox 360.

▶ *Guitar Hero 3: Legends of Rock* (2007) (PS2, PS3, Wii, Xbox 360, Windows, Mac, and mobile). This version allows for an online component with the PS3, Wii, and Xbox 360 to download additional songs if desired as well as compete against others over the network. Most library *Guitar Hero* tournaments are played against those in the actual room, not against those online. However, if your library has the capability, online play against other libraries can add a whole new level of competition to game play (note that only the PS3 allows play against random, rather than specific users). It has a higher difficulty level than the previous version, includes a battle mode where competition is not just about guitar play but about throwing objects at your opponent, and a loose storyline involving the players and nonplayable characters on the screen.

▶ *Guitar Hero 4: World Tour* (2008) (PS2, PS3, Wii, and Xbox 360). Vocals, bass, guitar, and drums are additions for game play. If your library already owns a copy of *Rock Band*, it would probably be too much duplication to purchase *Guitar Hero 4*. Music can be created and shared, and original music can be downloaded. If this is an area you want your library to venture into, consider music creation as a separate activity from the actual *Guitar Hero* tournament (which would require other software unless you have pretty tech- savvy and interested teens). Difficulty level is even higher than the previous versions, especially for chord sections.

▶ *Guitar Hero 5* (2009) (PS2, PS3, Wii, and Xbox 360). As in the previous version, this allows multiple instruments to be played. Players of various abilities can play together, including online. *Guitar Hero 5* includes challenges to unlock extras, such as characters, in the game.

Songs and Lyrics

Prior to game play, you can select which songs you want to allow (or not allow) for a tournament. The ESRB has given the *Guitar Hero* series a rating of T for Teen, which means it's appropriate for those 13 and older. The content descriptors include "mild lyrics" and "mild suggestive themes." Some songs may contain references to drugs or sex. If you feel this will be an issue for your library and the community, screen the lyrics beforehand and prominently display the game rating and appropriate ages. It also might be a great opportunity for some education about the content descriptors and the *Guitar Hero* game itself!

As mentioned earlier, songs are arranged by difficulty from lowest to highest. You will not want to select songs based on their lyrics only to find out they are not in the appropriate difficulty range for the tournament. Remember, selecting songs is optional; leaving it open to the players is also fine.

There are a couple time issues to consider. Most video game tournaments run on average two to three hours, so it's a good idea to screen the songs allowed based on how many minutes they are. If everyone wants to play Lynryd Skynyrd's "Free Bird," for example, be aware that it's close to ten minutes long. Most players would also appreciate having some practice time as part of the tournament. Usually 30 minutes is enough to play a few quick songs as well as to calibrate the notes with the projector if anything seems amiss with the timing.

Many songs will need to be unlocked before they can be played. If you have a memory card or know the code it is a good idea to save the game as you go. You can get codes from GameFAQs (www.gamfaqs.com, accessed 2009) with just a series of button presses on the guitar. It's a good idea to invite players with experience to help unlock the songs well before the day of the tournament. This will give some extra practice time and advertising as well! Because of the noise level, if unlocking songs needs to be done after hours, make sure when you are in the preparation state to schedule for this.

Set Game Parameters

Playing *Guitar Hero*

The game controllers for *Guitar Hero* are peripherals made to look like actual rock guitars. The Gibson Les Paul and Gibson SG, both electric guitars introduced in the 1950s and 1960s, respectively, are two models *Guitar Hero* uses for game play to numerous rock songs. The guitars on screen are even more numerous to choose from. Both lead and bass guitar tracks were added for *Guitar Hero 2*.

Guitars are available either wired (a cord that connects from the guitar to the console) or wireless. Both work fine for tournaments, although wireless gives players the ability to move around with more flair during game play. Wireless controllers usually require a peripheral called an "adapter" to achieve wireless capabilities that gets plugged into the console (or Wiimote in the guitar for the Wii).

Instead of strings, *Guitar Hero* guitars have five colored buttons (green, red, yellow, blue, and orange) to simulate frets and a whammy bar. Players watch a screen with scrolling colors that indicate the notes for the music. Players press the corresponding colored buttons on their controller to match the notes on the screen and to earn points. As the notes scroll across the screen, they pass over a specific area that instructs players to press the corresponding button. Players must simultaneously press the strum bar on the guitar as well. Points can be increased by playing ten notes consecutively. "Star Power" is earned by playing starred notes correctly and then activated by tilting the guitar upward, which can increase the performance meter and cause less penalty for notes that are missed.

If too many notes are missed during the game players may "fail" the song, as the rock meter will fall into the red zone and indicate "game over." The faster the notes scroll, the more of them there are at higher difficulty levels. Lower levels don't involve all of the notes to be played ("Easy" involves three notes, while "Hard" uses all five). Tournaments can be played in whatever difficulty level you choose, and it's important to specify this in your advertising and not pair a beginning-level player with someone who is way more advanced.

The colored notes aren't all that is on the screen. Some elaborate backdrops at venues such as theaters, bars, and high schools simulate actual play. They also include an attentive and cheering (sometimes booing!) crowd, stage lighting and pyrotechnics, and numerous stages detailed to feel like a rock concert. Billboards displaying ads even pop up throughout. If this is something your library may be concerned about, consider having a statement included in the advertising or just verbally mention before the tournament starts that "the views and opinions expressed in the ads are not those of this library." On-screen characters are modeled after rock stars from various genres. The newer the version of the game, the more detailed the costumes, hair, and lip-syncing animations have become.

Guitar Hero is now made to play with the Wii, PS2, PS3, Xbox 360, Nintendo DS, cell phones, and both Windows and Mac computing systems. If you have a choice as to what console to purchase for *Guitar Hero*, ask your patrons which console they prefer.

Rules and Regulations

The rules you set for your tournament, such as song length, duration of tournament, and approximate difficulty level, should be worked into an outline from which you and your volunteering expert can work out all the fine details. Make sure the event is fair for both beginning and advanced levels. If the tournament is not meant to be inclusive of all levels, then be very clear in your advertising who it is intended for. Running a parallel tournament for other levels, if staff and space allow, will help make the event more inclusive.

You will want to choose "Multiplayer" and then the "Face Off" mode for the actual tournament. Brackets such as the ones found at www.crowsdarts.com (accessed 2009) and http://gtsystem.org (accessed 2009; an online bracket system) can be used for a single- or double-elimination tournament. Basically, double means players get at least two tries to be the champion. Because your event must take place within a certain time period, if you allow double elimination, factor this, along with the lengths of the songs allowed for play, into your time frame. Putting a cap on the number of registrants (whether using single or double elimination) will help the event run more smoothly. Recording the score given at the end of game play is an easy and fair way to measure success (as long as the levels are the same because more points are given for more difficult levels and the songs are generally the same length).

Prizes

If your budget allows, prizes such as $25.00 gift certificates to local gaming stores are a great incentive for people to participate. Donations from gaming stores might be a possibility. Also consider library prizes such as free DVD rentals, extra computer time, or fine waivers.

Prepare for the Game

Plan for the Cost

Because most versions of *Guitar Hero* will play on any console, you have a lot of options if you need to buy one. Keep in mind that many stores sell used gaming consoles. Some libraries also have regular players bring their own equipment with a waiver indicating the library is not responsible for any damage that may incur.

If you do need to purchase a console, the cost will range roughly from $100.00 to $300.00. The game itself, depending on the version, can range from $25.00 for a basic one to $200.00 for a "deluxe" package. If the kit you decide to purchase doesn't come with the number of guitars that you want (probably two), you'll need to purchase them separately. Make sure your projector or television has adequate speakers. If you're going to use an online scoring system or project a score sheet during game play, you may need a laptop and additional projector and/or screens.

If you decide to have food, you'll need to budget for drinks or snacks ($25.00–$50.00) and paper products such as cups, plates, and napkins ($25.00–$30.00). You might even have leftovers to use at the next tournament!

Identify Space Needs

An enclosed room such as a library meeting room is an ideal place to hold a *Guitar Hero* event. If your library does not have an enclosed room, consider having an after-hours or outdoor event. Sometimes recreation centers will allow you to use their space, which can lead to a partnership of running events together in the future. If you need to adjust to a small space, a television or ceiling-mounted projector may do the trick. If possible, allow room for chairs or tables for viewers in addition to the players. Audience participation adds to the atmosphere of the tournament. Onlookers aren't absolutely necessary, but if a few can be accommodated, they add energy to the event. Be aware of the fire code and the room's capacity when you make this decision.

Make sure safety and security are accounted for especially in terms of equipment such as cords from the projector, television, and guitars connected to the consoles. Keeping the tournament area separate from the rest of the room (i.e., food, crowd) will go far in avoiding mishaps, especially in the middle of game play. If wireless controllers are used, most players will enjoy having the freedom to roam about the room to show off their performance flair, adding to the ambiance of the tournament.

Get Staff and Volunteers to Assist

It's best to run a *Guitar Hero* tournament with at least two staff. They can monitor crowd control, help keep score, and keep an eye out for the safety and security of the equipment, room, and participants. Don't underestimate the help your players will give you. Chances are they will help wherever they are needed because they too want the event to be a success. Consider putting the food table far from the gaming area with a volunteer assigned to monitor the area. Typical items include water, soda, and light snacks such as potato chips or granola bars. General rules can be announced in the advertising and mentioned during registration.

Plan for Other Activities in the Room

Game play with board or card games or even another console game can be run during practice time if your space allows. Don't choose a console game that is heavily dependent on noise as it will compete with *Guitar Hero*. Also avoid games such as *DDR* that take up a lot of room. A board, card, or console game that lasts about 30 minutes might help with crowd control as well as be an outlet for the nerves of the competing *Guitar Hero* players before the tournament.

Choose a Date and Time

Getting patron input for when to hold the *Guitar Hero* tournament is important. While room availability may be a limiting factor, as well as the library's policy against holding events after hours, at least you may be able to give your regulars some choice. Connecting the tournament to another program, such as summer reading kickoff or a music festival going on in your community, will add more focus and purpose to your event.

▶ INTEGRATE GAMING WITH AN ANIME FEST

Anime fests (also called anime cons, cosplays (costume play), and anime afternoons) take place in many libraries throughout the country. They are inspired by AnimeFest (www.animefest.org), a gaming convention and organization, founded in 1992 and based in Dallas, TX, for fans of Japanese pop culture, including animation (anime), music, and manga (comics).

Libraries That Participated in an Anime Fest in 2009

Broward County Library, Florida
www.broward.org/library
Evansville Vanderburgh, Indiana
www.evpl.org
Hennepin County Library, Minnesota
www.hclib.org
Northside Branch, Lexington Public Library, Kentucky
www.lexpublib.org
Sarnia Branch Library, Lambton County Library, Ontario Canada
www.lclmg.org
Yardley-Makefield Branch Library, Bucks County Free Library, Pennsylvania
www.buckslib.org

Video games, card games, and "game-like" activities such as dance-offs or random battles are often a central part of an anime fest. Cosplay, where people come dressed in costumes from their favorite anime, manga, or even video game, is also a big part of an anime fest (although many anime fests do occur without people coming dressed in costume). Anime fests differ from anime clubs in that there are usually a variety of activities, not just movie viewing or discussions about manga. The fests tend to be a special event that might happen once or a few times a year rather than monthly or weekly. Although the fests may pull in members of a club that regularly meets at the library, they will probably garner a lot more attendees than just the "regulars."

Identify Your Target Audience

Libraries have reported that attendance varies across the board in terms of gender, ethnicity, and age. Some libraries reported having more middle school boys show up at the anime book club while more high school females attended the anime fest. Others said that it's really split 50–50 in terms of gender.

In terms of age range, several libraries reported a noticeable age difference at first (middle and high school), but as the same kids keep attending, they all learn the ropes for how the event goes and the age gap doesn't seem as important to them. Some libraries hold anime fests just for teens, while others open it to all ages to encourage families to attend. One library reported that a parent was grateful to have the opportunity to attend an event about something she knew her daughter enjoyed. It is not uncommon to have the 20-to-35-year-old crowd attend an anime fest if it's open to all ages.

One librarian said that her anime fest really brought in a diverse range of cultural groups. Because anime has such a universal following, it is natural that it might cross boundaries in ways that other programs don't.

Whatever activities you ultimately decide to have at the anime fest, don't underestimate your patrons' enthusiasm in wanting to help set it up. If you view them as the experts, particularly when it comes to the details of what games they want and what activities they like, chances are the participants will be much more engaged and their excitement for the event will carry over to other potential attendees.

Choose the Game

Video Games at an Anime Fest

The socialization factor is a key ingredient of any anime fest, so games should be multiplayer (i.e., two to four or more players).

The ability for a group to play and physically interact outweighs whether the content of the game has crossover with anime or manga. Fast-paced games where matches last only a few minutes are also generally more suitable for play. Here are six popular crossover video games that lend themselves well to an anime fest for their social interaction and fast-paced play:

1. *Naruto* (with well over 20 spinoffs generally rated either T for Teen or Everyone 10+)
2. *Final Fantasy* (over 30 in the series and generally rated T, E for Everyone, or Everyone 10+)
3. *Pokémon* (over 30 and rated E for Everyone)
4. *Super Smash Brothers* (*Brawl* and *Melee* are the most popular and rated T for Teen)
5. *Dance Dance Revolution* (over 20 and rated E for Everyone)
6. *Mario Kart* (rated E for Everyone)

Most of these games have online play capabilities. If libraries want to play against each other online, you will just have to coordinate a time to link up online through the game. However, make sure you're comfortable with what the online option entails (a live port, strong connection not firewalled, and sometimes extra peripherals such as a LAN adapter for the Wii). I would not recommend that you choose an anime fest as your first foray into going online. You don't want online play to become a negative focal point if a lot of technical troubleshooting is needed, which would cause a lag and bring the game performance down.

Consoles for these games span the range of Wii, PS2, PS3, and Xbox 360. *Pokémon* is played mainly on handhelds such as the Game Boy Advance and Nintendo DS (players can be encouraged to bring their own). *Mario Kart*, which allows up to four players, is usually a hit with middle schoolers and intuitive enough for first-time gamers to pick up quickly. The game can be physically active, especially if players like to use the Wiimote inside the steering wheel to race their vehicle on the screen.

DDR was first introduced in Japan in the late 1990s, so its crossover with anime is a natural fit and popular at most festivals. It is a very physical game as well, where players step on a platform with colored arrows that correspond to scrolling arrows on the screen. Moves are in succession and combined, so they can be very fast and take a lot of coordination. If cosplay is part of your anime fest, make sure outfits or props won't be a hindrance or a danger for quick-footed *DDR* players.

Open play is probably the best arrangement for any of the listed games rather than creating a tournament. While gaming still might be a focal point for your event, depending on your audience, a less formal structure will encourage attendees to participate in other activities spread throughout the anime fest. With an open structure, it is easier to promote related books by displaying them around the playing area as kids go from station to station.

Card Games at an Anime Fest

Magic: The Gathering, Yu-Gi-Oh!, and Pokémon are staple card games at anime fests. *Magic: The Gathering* was discussed in depth earlier in this chapter.

Yu-Gi-Oh! is an action/adventure/fantasy Japanese manga created in the early 1990s. Chances are your library will have copies to check out for the Anime Fest, including issues of *Shonen Jump* magazine, where readers can get their fill of Yu-Gi-Oh the character (aka, The King of Games). Board, card, and video games have been made from parts of the Yu-Gi-Oh! series. The trading card game by the same name as the manga series is published by Konami. The object of the game is to reduce a player's life points by playing cards that will "attack" opponents.

Both casual and tournament play is common with trading cards. Participants may bring their own decks, or, if funding allows, you can plan to have some available. Starter decks run about $4.00 each. You should get a sense of whether the majority of your Yu-Gi-Oh! players will be brand new to the game or more experienced, as this will determine the type of deck to purchase. Because most casual game play with the Yu-Gi-Oh! trading cards is short (less than 30 minutes), it lends itself well as a side activity during an anime fest. The game is recommended for those ages seven and older and for two to four players (www.boardgamegeek.com/boardgame/4154, accessed 2009).

Pokémon, like Yu-Gi-Oh!, is a popular video game and anime, manga, and trading card game. The trading card game is published by Wizards of the Coast (www.wizards.com, accessed 2009), which also publishes *Magic: The Gathering*. The Pokémon trading cards and video game are both great components to most any library's anime fest. The general object of the game is to collect other Pokémon species and train them to battle against others. Pokémon gamers tend to be middle school males, but this can definitely vary from one community to another. Once they are in high school, Pokémon fans typically take up playing the *Super Smash Brothers* video game (Wii). *Super Smash Brothers* has many of the same Pokémon characters, which makes it also a popular activity with Japanese tie-ins to the anime fest. The duration of a Pokémon card game can vary, lasting generally 20–30 minutes. It supports the socialization factor because it's made for up to four players and is recommended for those as young as six to seven years old (www.boardgamegeek.com/boardgame/2165, accessed 2009).

Other Gaming Activities at an Anime Fest

Activities related to gaming at an anime fest typically go beyond the obvious—card, board, or video games. Cosplay, random battles, and dance offs are all related to gaming in their own way and will be explored further.

Cosplay. While it's a bit of a stretch to say that cosplay itself is a game, it does have a relationship with gaming. Cosplay in the context of an anime fest usually means wearing a costume related to the games themselves. Because there is a lot of crossover with manga, anime, and video games, it is not uncommon for participants to come dressed as video game characters such as Naruto or as a character from *Final Fantasy* and *Kingdom Hearts*. Some libraries may opt to provide equipment such as a sewing machine and material to help participants construct their clothes. Making accessories such as Naruto's headband or tight-fitting face mask can also be on-the-spot activities that don't require sewing.

If you would like to undertake the activity of helping with the construction of clothes or props before the actual anime fest, involve your participants first. If they have little or no expertise or equipment, you might opt for designing a few props rather than full regalia. Investigate a partnership in the community—perhaps with a sewing store or students in a fashion design program at a local school. Sometimes libraries have partnerships with hair salons, especially around prom events. Engaging a salon to re-create hair styles for specific characters is a surefire way to help participants with their overall look. Commercial Web sites such as Cosplay Ninja (www.cosplayninja.com, accessed 2009) sell ready-made costumes. You may be able to help attendees find a similar pattern at a local sewing store they can modify with the help of a seamstress and a few lessons.

Define permissible materials for props and accessories. Avoid metallic objects and anything that is sharp or has spikes or protrusions that may accidentally poke or injure someone. Take a look at the clothing policies of past anime conventions to see what is generally acceptable. While conventions are on a much larger scale than your anime fest, their protocols give a helpful heads-up on issues to be aware of. A good place to start looking is the Anime Convention Nexus Web site (www.animecons.com, accessed 2009), which compiles anime conventions in the United States and beyond and provides links to individual sites. These are typical and permissible costume materials:

▶ Foam core
▶ Cardboard
▶ Styrofoam
▶ Plastic
▶ Fabric
▶ Clay (especially for jewelry)

Attendees will want their costumes and accessories to look realistic. This is where you can come in with resources and supplies to help make their experience a successful one. These resources offer tips and step-by-step instructions on how to develop props and accessories for a cosplay-themed anime fest, as well as an insight into event logistics and supplemental activities:

▶ Cosplay Classes (www.cosplayclasses.com, accessed 2009)
   This blog is a great hands-on site with video tutorials, downloadable patterns, and links to sites with additional cosplay information.
▶ "Get with the Program: Godzilla vs. The Librarian" (http://pdfs.voya.com/VO/YA2/VOYA200608GetProgram.pdf, accessed 2009)

This 2006 VOYA article by Kevin A.R. King highlights activities for anime fests in libraries, including several that have had successful cosplay events—including an anime prom!

▶ Teen Alternative Fashion Show (http://vimeo.com/6725515, accessed 2009)

In 2006, the Fayetteville Public Library in Arkansas held a fashion show for teens and by teens during Teen Read Week. Many of their creations were reflective of characters that would be seen at an anime fest.

An easy way to create a costume for cosplay is to alter an existing garment. Altering clothes such as T-shirts and old hand-me-downs are a cheap and easy way to ensure full participation. These books can help get those creative juices flowing in terms of altering existing clothes:

▶ *Altered Clothing: Hip Fixes and Transformations with a Needle and Thread*, by Kathleen Maggio (Quarry Books, 2006)
▶ *Rip It!: How to Deconstruct and Reconstruct the Clothes of Your Dreams*, by Elissa Meyrich (Fireside, 2006)
▶ *Generation T: 108 Ways to Transform a T-Shirt*, by Megan Nicolay (Workman Publishing, 2006)

Random Battles. Cosplay can involve much more than just putting on a costume and wearing it to an event. Role playing is a common activity for an anime fest. Some libraries include what is called "random battles." In this game-like activity, participants are in the center of the room, or at least in a marked-off area, and act out a scene from a book, movie, or video game.

While a stage area isn't necessary, you'll want to have a decent amount of space for random battles. The participants need to be able to freely move around, with the audience either facing them or forming a circle around them. Participants then role-play a brief scene that most of the attendees are familiar with. They win points for staying true to character and lose points for falling out of character. An opponent is considered "defeated" if he or she is "attacked" or "killed" with a signature move by the other. Have your participants come up with the rules (or at least be the judges), if you think there will be a lot of interest for such an activity at your library event.

Random battles are flexible and do not have to involve costumes. It might be more fun if costumes are worn, but those who don't dress up should not be excluded. You will want to put a 30- to 45-minute time limit on the event, as participants may want to continue role playing long after the event is over! Registration for random battles is encouraged, especially if you're implementing a structured timeline.

Dance Offs. Dance offs are another game-like activity that libraries include as part of their anime fests. Most kids like to mimic the moves of their favorite characters. This activity is a contest based on dances that take place in anime movies before the show starts. You will want a projector, speakers, and screen to display the video for those unfamiliar with it. More experienced dancers can be at the front to demonstrate the moves, but the projection will demonstrate moves on a larger scale.

> A helpful resource is the article *The Anime-ted Library* by Kat Kan and Kristin Fletcher-Spear (http://pdfs.voya.com/VO/YA2/VOYA200504 AnimetedLibrary.pdf, accessed 2009).

Prizes such as a gift certificate for the "craziest interpretation," "most humorous," or "best dancer" can be awarded to keep the event fun and light rather than a serious competition. Like random battles, you should have a time limit and plenty of space for the entire group to participate. If you do not have a lot of space, consider having dance offs interspersed throughout the event where participants can rotate between dancing and judging.

Prepare for the Game

Anime fests can be as big or as small as you want them, depending on the activities you feel are most appropriate and will be well received at your library. Generally, a community room can support a variety of activities going on simultaneously, such as video games, food, board or card games, and an area for random battles, dance offs, or cosplay.

Make sure you have enough staff to run the activities. An emcee and photographer can help add excitement and energy. Other staff or volunteers can help serve food. Japanese-themed food such as mochi, sesame crackers, and pocky are a fun and easy way to introduce kids to food from a different culture. Keeping this food away from any gaming equipment is a good idea.

You may even decide to allow manga, anime, and related materials to be checked out during your anime fest. If so, provide library card applications and enough staff (one or two) to help facilitate this service.

▶ BEGIN A CIRCULATING GAME COLLECTION

A great selling point for using the library's budget money to purchase equipment for a gaming tournament is that afterward you can reuse the gaming equipment to begin a circulating game collection. While the primary goal was to organize a one-time gaming event, the secondary goal could be to support an ongoing effort to boost library membership through a circulating games collection.

Fortunately, many issues surrounding beginning a circulating game collection are the same issues as running a gaming tournament, so implementing both services practically go hand in hand. The main difference is that you will have to devise a way for patrons to check equipment out and return it without damage. The other issues are discussed in Chapter 2.

Provide Staff Training

Getting the approval to have a collection at your library is the first step; building, managing, and sustaining the collection are the next. Staff training will likely be necessary because the level of knowledge the staff have about gaming will vary. If some staff are very knowledgeable about gaming, use their expertise to develop training resources for the less knowledgeable staff. Training tips can include where to order materials, which consoles go with which games, knowing when and how to weed a collection, and keeping up-to-date with current gaming policies and procedures. Any reports or presentations with any changes to policies should be kept with the training resources, as well.

Some staff may not be aware that certain games only play on certain consoles. While many games are now made for a variety of platforms, some still remain proprietary to one console. If your library has made the decision to circulate games, make sure the games can be played on whichever console you purchase, and find out if they are compatible on multiple platforms. Try to find real-life photo examples of what platforms (e.g., PS2, PS3, Wii, Xbox 360) the games are compatible with, and look for this information when ordering them or reading their reviews.

Many libraries have flexibility with their budget in terms of ordering procedures. The funding for your video gaming collection may come with stipulations of where the games must be purchased. Sometimes libraries can use credit cards at local stores such as Best Buy, GameStop, Target, or Walmart, which also will likely sell used games at a lower rate. Most jobbers such as Baker & Taylor (www.btol.com, accessed 2009; which also provides a list of new releases for the year well ahead of when they are due out), Ingram (www.ingrambook.com, accessed 2009), and BWi (www.bwibooks.com, accessed 2009) carry video games and are already familiar places to most libraries ordering gaming materials. These companies are a good place to start when purchasing video games, as they are safe and reliable. Suggesting an unfamiliar source for video games may turn out to be more complicated for new staff ordering for the first time.

Chances are your library already stocks gaming magazines such as *GamePro* (www.gamepro.com, accessed 2009), *Game Informer* (www.gameinformer.com, accessed 2009) and *Nintendo Power* (www.nintendopower.com, accessed 2009) that carry game reviews. Be aware, though, that by the time the magazine is processed and on the shelves at your library, the game you may want to order is considered "old" or out-of-date. For this reason, you should also consult online sites such as GameRankings (www.gamerankings.com, accessed 2009) and Metacritic (www.metacritic.com, accessed 2009). The online counterparts of the magazines mentioned earlier carry reviews as well.

Last, invite administrators and staff to play the games periodically in the staff lounge. Many of us don't hesitate to read the latest book in the collection. We can then pass on our recommendation to others. This is what readers advisory groups are all about. We usually don't just read the reviews and then not the book itself (unless pressed for time). The readers advisory concept isn't usually applied in the same way to video games. Several librarians have reported that many patrons just take a game off the shelf, not really caring about the title as long as it matches the console they have at home.

The learning curve will be a bit steeper for some video games than for others, and most people will probably not have enough time to play the game all the way through. However, that's not always necessary to get a feel for what the game is about. The game's goal and how to play it are easy to pick up and are useful bits of information to whoever might be evaluating the game.

Inviting staff or administration to gaming events can also be a way to bring exposure to gaming in libraries. Being able to observe firsthand the mentorship that takes place, the conversations about library services and materials, and the learning potential that comes with becoming a skillful game player are all valuable points. Observing gaming in action can help entice staff into wanting to know more about the collection and ultimately bring them onboard. Also, many patrons might be happy to share their interest and knowledge about games with staff. This kind of relationship will help strengthen the overall sense of community and keep library staff in touch with their patrons' needs and desires.

Establish Circulation Parameters

Duration of Checkout

Limiting the number of games that can be checked out per card and how long they can be checked out will put the brakes on potential theft. Keep in mind that it can take a long time (approximately 10–15 hours) to be able to master every level of a game. This doesn't mean that everyone who checks out a game is going to want to play every level before returning it, but it can be cause to allow extra time for checkouts—perhaps up to three weeks. Some libraries limit checkout time to three days, and they limit the number of games that can be checked out per card or per day to one to three. Again, given that it can take many hours to play through a game, keeping the numbers low on what can be checked out is fair. How many games your budget allows for purchase and for replacement will also dictate how many games should be allowed to be checked out at any given time per card, per household.

Many libraries that have circulating video game collections rarely interlibrary loan them. While the games may still fly off the shelves at your library, not allowing them to be loaned out to remote libraries can help the collection be more responsive to your local community.

Fines and Fees

Generally, late fees range from a quarter to $1.00 for video games. You may establish them to be on par with the collection fees already in place for the audiovisual collection. Although fines are important because they encourage responsibility for the library's materials, you don't want fine collecting to become a burden on staff.

As you go along, periodically review the policies you put in place, so you'll become aware if and when they should be altered. For example, slightly longer checkout times may ease up the need to collect late fees. Limiting the number of games that can be checked out when a certain fee is reached on a library card, no matter what format, may also be an option. Ordering multiple copies of particular games that are more frequently checked out is a great response that may help cut down on fines. Some libraries occasionally have "food for fines" days where patrons bring in canned goods to remove all or part of their library card fines, which is something that may work for overdue games. A variation is to have a "games for fines" day, where patrons bring in old games to become part of the library's circulating collection in trade for library fines.

►4

MARKETING

► Get the Word Out in Print and Online
► Use Ongoing and Live Marketing Techniques
► Engage in Both Marketing and Promotion
► Get to Know "The Gamers"
► Offer Readers Advisory Support for Gamers
► Promote Your Specific Gaming Program

Now that you have determined what type of gaming program you want to implement at your library, you'll need to let everyone in on the details. Libraries market programs all of the time; your gaming program is no different.

► GET THE WORD OUT IN PRINT AND ONLINE

Prepublicity Considerations

Before reaching out to teens and youth, find out how they communicate with each other. Online? Word of mouth? Text messaging? According to an August 2009 report from Pew Internet & American Life, in 2008, 71 percent of teens age 12–17 owned a mobile phone. In 2004, the figure was 45 percent (Pew Internet, www .pewinternet.org/~/media//Files/Reports/2009/PIP%20Teens %20and%20Mobile%20Phones%20Data%20Memo.pdf, accessed 2009). Libraries should be aware of trends in order to stay in touch with their patrons' evolving needs and wants.

Additionally, you will also need to decide if you want to target the casual gamer or the hard-core gamer. For the hard-core gamer, you might skip the clip art and use actual screenshots and terminology of the particular game in your publicity.

Traditional Print Marketing

Most libraries use flyers to advertise a new service or program (see Figure 4.1). Flyers usually consist of attractive and bright colors

▶ Figure 4.1: Gaming Flyer

and are posted around the library, particularly in the department most frequented by the target audience. You may even put up a book display with gaming-related peripherals, such as controllers and board game boards, to draw more attention to a posted flyer. Other ways to publicize the program are through newsletters, ads in school papers, and notices in other community print materials.

It may sound obvious, but it's important to include the appropriate contact information of the department running the program, and make sure that the other departments have a basic knowledge about it. Most libraries have a standard format for creating flyers that includes the who, what, where, when, and how of the event as well as the library's logo. It's always a good idea to have someone else look over the print materials to make sure the information is correct. This is especially important with gaming programs, because gaming in the library might not seem like an obvious library program. If patrons have any questions, don't let the lack of contact information be their first impression about the new library gaming program!

Keep in mind that the audience for the flyers might be different from the audience of your program, as library-related program flyers are typically picked up by adults and parents. That's not to say that your marketing shouldn't be geared toward youth and teens, but just be aware you want to appeal to as many different library patron subcategories as possible.

A flyer can have a lot of information on it, yet say little. If the impression is that the library doesn't know what it's talking about, that is, if the title of a game is spelled incorrectly or the character depicted on the flyer is from a different game, participants will not expect the event to be worthwhile. Don't be afraid to get feedback from your intended audience about a flyer you're creating. They might even have a flair for designing flyers themselves. This can be a great opportunity to put creative literacy skills to work!

Traditional Online Marketing

Traditional print advertising shares many similarities with online marketing. Your library likely has a URL and other relevant sites that can be listed on the flyer. Many libraries may be able to add the flyer directly to their Web sites.

Many libraries use social networking sites on a regular basis, such as MySpace (www.myspace.com, accessed 2009), Facebook (www.facebook.com, accessed 2009), Twitter (www.twitter.com, accessed 2009), and blogs (www.wordpress.com, accessed 2009), where the information can be posted and shared. The benefit of using such Web sites is the ability to quickly and easily post or send information. They also provide opportunities for online contacts to interact with you about the event by posting questions and leaving comments.

Sometimes school libraries block these sites, particularly middle and high school libraries. In such cases, an intranet site may be a great alternative. Making the program part of daily school announcements or however other programs and clubs are typically announced at the school (posters in the hallway or closed circuit TV) can be done as well and are all great ways to give gaming its deserved place as a "normal" and core service or activity. Be sure to invite teachers to attend the event as well; it is an opportunity for teachers and students to relate to one another outside the classroom.

Forums Boards and Other Web Sites

Don't ignore posting your event on the Web sites where fans of the game or activity frequent. Expecting people to find the information only inside your library or on your library Web site will shortchange yourself and your audience. If you're having a tournament game with *DDR*, for example, DDR Freak (www.ddrfreak.com, accessed 2009) has an extensive forums board with information about tournaments and events from all over the United States and beyond. Posting an event here lets the already existing community know that you know they exist and are meeting them where they already hang out, so to speak.

Board Game Geek (www.boardgamegeek.com, accessed 2009) has a place where the details of gaming conventions or gaming groups throughout the world can be posted. This might be another opportunity to advertise and promote your event to a fan base in your area.

If your activity involves geocaching, you'll definitely want to promote it on geocaching.com (www.geocaching.com, accessed 2009), which is a central Web site where geocaching fans go to find out what caches are hidden near them. geocaching.com uses a template to automatically assign you a moderator who checks your work to make sure it is accurate and answers any questions you might have. The template might take a little navigating at first, especially if this is your first foray into the sport, but the moderator will help you along. You fill the template in with information about your hidden caches, including details about the terrain where the caches are hidden, such as accessibility. Posting on the official geocaching site will also help you learn what information is important to include on your own library's site as well.

Not all games have an obvious forums board, but for the ones that do, it is a great way to connect with others. If you're not sure if your particular event has a fan site, don't hesitate to ask those you know who might be familiar with the activity or game.

▶ USE ONGOING AND LIVE MARKETING TECHNIQUES

Have postcard-sized handouts with URLs, phone numbers, or other contact information to give out whenever you can. Simply handing out your business cards (including mobile business cards and MOO cards) and making a brief introduction before the program starts of where people can find more information can help.

Take videos with a handheld recorder such as the Flip (http://theflip.com, accessed 2009) or RCA's Small Wonder (www.mysmallwonder.com, accessed 2009) or photographs with a digital camera and post them live on the Internet during the event. Because you won't have a lot of time to do much editing, take short clips and just make sure you have a computer or laptop ready with the program software installed that is needed, depending on the camera you are using. If your library has a policy about getting permission for taking photos and/or video, do this at the point of sign-in or registration before the event if possible.

Showing your event live on the Internet helps make attendees feel part of something larger. You can do this by blogging through such Web sites as CoverItLive (www.coveritlive.com, accessed 2009), twittering (www.twitter.com accessed 2009), updating an RSS feed, or streaming (www.ustream.tv, accessed 2009). If you want to allow others to contribute to live blogging or twittering, which means publishing the attendees' comments about what is going on right at the moment, you'll need a laptop and projector. Show the Web site on a wall during the event so people can friend you and join in by texting from their cell phones. Depending on the library's phone plan, you might want a disclaimer that the library is not responsible for any texting charges that may incur.

To stream an event using a Web site like Ustream (www.ustream.tv), you need a Webcam (built-in or purchased) and a free account with Ustream. The Webcam captures and records the event live. People can also text chat, if enabled, to have a conversation about what they're watching. The camera can be pointed at the game play as well as the crowd. Some people enjoy watching others play an exciting gaming match!

For a great step-by-step blog post on how to use Ustream, check out librarian Joseph Wilk's blog post about recording an online gaming tournament (http://yalsa.ala.org/blog/2008/07/23/ program-planning-online-brawl-tournaments/#more-1269, accessed 2009).

Having an archive of the stream is another way to continue advertising the event after the fact and show what a great time it was. Don't forget that the follow-up of the event (photos, videos, commentary) can be used in advertising for future events.

Text messaging is a popular way to send and receive information quickly, and many youth communicate this way. If you're looking to experiment with text messaging a select group of people, consider Mozes (www.mozes.com, accessed 2009), where you can set up a free "mob" or mobile list that people can opt in to join and receive your messages, or Broadtexter (www.broadtexter.com, accessed 2009), which is free and alerts people about your event. Charges for texting do apply, so libraries may want to include a disclaimer that they are not responsible for any fees that may incur. Guide by Cell (www.guidebycell.com, accessed 2009) sells mobile advertising packages to organizations such as libraries.

▶ ENGAGE IN BOTH MARKETING AND PROMOTION

Marketing a program is when we post flyers or program information in print materials or online via different Web sites. Promoting a program is when we develop a more personal relationship with our target audience, though this does not necessarily mean a direct face-to-face invite is required. In general, once you've determined your target audience, you will want to:

- ▶ Know some information about the software or game and what other activities will be available. Is it a physical game, something quick to learn and easy to play? What skills are being learned? You can then talk about this information with your patrons.
- ▶ Be open to suggestions of activities to add to the event. Once you start talking about the program, people might share their own thoughts about "what might be really cool" to do. They may even want to help get the word out.
- ▶ Be open to talking about the event with partners or contacts who might not seem obvious at first. A casual invitation to "come hang out," which truly is not out of place at most gaming events, is a way to attract people with different perspectives to participate.

To spread the word about the gaming program at my library, I took a *Dance Dance Revolution* game to the nearby high school, where the students were allowed to play it during their lunch hour and in the halls before their next classes. The crowds enjoyed watching their fellow students show off their skills so much that the principal ended up telling the students to get to class after the competition. This type of promotion definitely got the students excited about the library's gaming program. I also found that the school was very supportive of this lunchtime activity.

▶ GET TO KNOW "THE GAMERS"

Gaming is one of those activities that are both a hands-on and a spectator sport. Those who don't describe themselves as "gamers" might miss out on enjoying the activity if the event sounds like it's only for a select few or that technical know-how is required.

In a class offered by Infopeople (http://infopeople.org) in summer 2009 about intergenerational gaming, one of the assignments was to interview an older adult and a teen about gaming.

Most of the responses indicated that the older adult (and in many cases the teen) didn't use the term "gamer" to describe themselves. But, when prodded further about examples of games they might play, they definitely responded positively to the activity.

▶ OFFER READERS ADVISORY SUPPORT FOR GAMERS

One way to spread the word about the library's gaming program is through a readers advisory group. Discovering the kind of books your patrons like to read and connecting what they're reading with the games they're playing can go a long way in learning how to highlight your library's gaming program.

Beth Gallaway, library consultant and author of *Game On! Gaming at the Library* (Neal-Schuman, 2009), gives great tips on readers advisory for gamers as part of the Gaming in Libraries course for Syracuse University (www.gamesinlibraries.org/course/?p=176, accessed 2009). Don't panic if patrons mention a game that you know nothing about. Ask them for more information! You don't know about every single book or author in your library either. It helps to have a working knowledge about the games in your gaming program so that you can talk intelligently about them and sound confident about your program.

Asking patrons what it is they like best about a particular game will also give you a better understanding of what a parallel read might be. Don't forget about other formats such as movies, graphic novels, audiobooks, and magazines. Browsing through gaming magazines when the new issue comes in can also help you keep up-to-date and give you more information to talk about with others as it comes up.

▶ PROMOTE YOUR SPECIFIC GAMING PROGRAM

We've talked about a wide variety of gaming programs throughout this book, especially in Chapter 3. The type of program you have will often determine the kind of advertising you would want to do. For example, if you're having a game design program using a particular software program, design a simple game or have a volunteer design one that is playable *and* advertises your program. Add it to your library's Web site and other online sites your library might be connected with.

Scholar Marshall McLuhan is known for saying, "the medium is the message." This phrase definitely applies here. In other words, if patrons are interested in the program and see examples of what they would be learning in the promotional message, chances are they will be interested in attending. They may also feel they will be participating in a top-notch program when they can see the library is a place where content can be created. A few ideas in this vein are suggested below for advertising specific gaming programs.

Monthly Video Game Tournament

How you promote your event can often make or break it. First, consider your audience. If your tournament is aimed at tweens, MySpace would probably not be an appropriate venue to advertise, but a blog where they can comment might be. If you're trying to attract nonlibrary users, you'll need to move beyond your library's Web site and post your event on the gaming sites themselves. For example, if your tournament game is *Madden 09*, go to the EA Sports Forums at http://forum.ea.com/eaforum/categories/show/83.page (accessed 2009) and post your information. Fans of the game will notice your post.

Connect with the community that your target market is a member of. If you are targeting adults, getting permission to advertise at a local sports restaurant or bar would be appropriate. For a school-age audience, connecting with teachers—and not just the librarians—will help you get the word out about a safe, free, and friendly event open to all.

Ask teens for their expertise in helping to create a promotional video for the tournament. Chances are they would love to help, and advertising generated by peers is much more effective than anything that can come from staff. Make sure the video lives on more than just your library's Web site. Both YouTube and Facebook can help get the word out fast. Don't be afraid to continually build on your base audience. Take notes as you get good ideas or suggestions, and then try them out each month!

Sometimes the game itself can help advertise the actual event. If you're going to have a *Rock Band* tournament, perhaps there are a few days or even weeks leading up to the fest during which players can experience open play or just casual gaming with no competition. Giving participants a chance to hone their skills at home so they can impress everyone come tournament time will likely get players more aware and interested. They can then help you by spreading the word themselves.

Board Game Advertising

Use your library's networks—those that are popular with your target audience. If you're advertising on MySpace and the age group for your tournament is too young, come up with other options. Your library's blog and Web site, flyers, and word of mouth are all great ways to get the word out. Post announcements at a local gaming store or an online forum for the game. Board Game Geek (www.boardgamegeek.com, accessed 2009) has a tournament forums board as well as reviews, ratings, and a wealth of information about thousands of board games.

Find out if there is a convention (or con) in your area. You can usually do this at a local board game store. Cons are events where a variety of board games, especially role-playing games, are introduced and demonstrated for attendees. It might be a place to attract fans to your event as well as share information about the library. Often con organizers are grateful for community participation, which might include being able to set up a table and host a game or simply have library resources present that make a connection with the particular con.

Board games can also be tied into a school's curriculum. Brian Mayer (a librarian gamer) examined how board games connect to both the AASL Standards for the 21st-Century Learner (new school library standards) and New York State educational standards (http:// sls.gvboces.org/gaming/node/23.cfm, accessed 2009). Talk with teachers about the connections that can be made between board games and school library standards, and demonstrate the game at the school either in meetings or by having it available in the staff lounge. You might even invite teachers to an afterschool event in the library.

Magic: The Gathering

Contact the local high school to see if you can distribute flyers or put up posters in the common areas. Partner with a local game shop if you intend to pursue *Magic* as a continuing program. Post on the library's Facebook or MySpace page as well. If a librarian is a DCI judge (that is, he or she obtained a certificate from Wizards of the Coast to judge sanctioned *Magic* tournaments), then have the librarian post the event on the Wizards' Web site. It has a nice dropdown menu by state about what's going on where and one for pre-release parties (www.wizards.com/Magic/Magazine/Article .aspx?x=mtgcom/events/prereleases, accessed 2009).

Guitar Hero

Flyers, social networking sites (Facebook, MySpace, YouTube, etc.), and word of mouth are all viable ways to promote your event. The more you can get the players themselves involved in spreading the word, the better chance you will get a lot of excited attendees. Don't forget the *Guitar Hero* forums (http://hub.guitarhero.com/ stage/tournament, accessed 2009), where fans often look to see what events are happening online. Often local gaming stores, schools, or after-school clubs would be happy to help promote your library's *Guitar Hero* fest, as well.

Cosplay

Because gaming at cosplay events is usually intended to be very social, getting participants involved in planning the event is a great way to raise awareness about the event. If people are helping organize the event, they will be more invested in wanting it to be a success so they will likely invite their friends to come as well. If there are local anime cons, their help can play a big part in advertising and bringing people to the event. Take a look at the success Wake County Libraries in North Carolina have had at anime cons from this YALSA blog post: http://yalsa.ala.org/blog/2009/05/25/ how-to-sponsor-a-manga-library-at-an-anime-con (accessed 2009).

Be open to new ways to market and promote your program the next time around. Don't feel you need to get everything right the first time. If you're applying for a grant for a gaming program, don't forget to include funds for marketing. Develop a brand name and logo for your program, if it's intended to be an annual or repeated event. However, nothing can replace word-of-mouth marketing. We're much more likely to attend an event if our peers recommend it. Your program will speak for itself if you lay the groundwork for it to be successful.

▶5

BEST PRACTICES

- ▶ Use Gaming to Encourage Learning
- ▶ Organize a Gaming Career Night
- ▶ Support Gaming Groups for All Ages
- ▶ Learn from the Best Practices of Other Librarians
- ▶ Develop Your Own Best Practices

In this chapter, we'll examine best practices for gaming programs in a variety of different libraries. The following examples are meant to illustrate the risks and the rewarding benefits of implementing a new gaming program. While the programs that are highlighted took place in either a school, academic, or public library, the different aspects of each program can easily be adapted to any type of library.

▶ USE GAMING TO ENCOURAGE LEARNING

Gaming in a School Library: Summer School Style

Diana, a teacher–librarian at a public elementary school in Ontario, taught a three-week summer school session for seventh and eighth graders. Her class was based on literacy and numeracy. She chose to focus the subject matter on gaming, particularly because she sensed that the students didn't want to be there in the summer and this would make it more enjoyable. She was right.

In preparation, she sought permission to install RuneScape (www.runescape.com, accessed 2009), an online role-playing game, on the library computers. While she was allowed to use the computers for the class, she wasn't given permission to have anything extra installed on them. She was given some praise at the school for wanting to try something different to motivate the students.

Diana was flexible in her plan to use games to motivate the students. All of her original plan wasn't supported, so she created some workarounds for the students to still be able to participate according to the original concept of gaming. In the future, if Diana has the opportunity to continue the program, perhaps installing programs on flash drives and running them on the networked computers might be an option for her class and the administrators.

To set the tone of the class, Diana had the students read an excerpt from *Got Game: How the Gamer Generation Is Reshaping Business Forever*, by John C. Beck and Mitchell Wade (Harvard Business Press, 2004), who used gaming as an example to show what persuasive writing looks like. Diana says, "I hoped that not only would the students learn how to write different forms of non-fiction text better, they would also learn how to advocate for their own preferred learning styles and justify the forms of entertainment they enjoyed to authority figures" (e-mail interview, August 2009).

In addition to traditional reading, writing, and mathematical activities, the students also played a variety of online games that did not require being installed on the computers. *Set Game* (www .setgame.com, accessed 2009) helped them recognize number patterns and build algebra skills. In this game, players choose a set, which means three cards have to be all the same or different in color, pattern, or shape. In *Kingdom of Loathing* (www .kingdomofloathing.com, accessed 2009), students created characters that would participate in quests that involved following text-based narratives.

Last, the students played the *Lemonade Game* (www .lemonadegame.com, accessed 2009) where they became entrepreneurs by taking on the role of salespeople, developing a backstory for their character, and learning how to stay in business based on decisions they made about their lemonade. Traditional ways of exploring mathematical concepts were woven into their online games, such as when they worked with charts in their math books to record sales results for their recipes.

Other games that weren't computer based included Risk 2210 A.D. (www.boardgamegeek.com/boardgame/1829, accessed 2009), which is set in the future, is based on machines in battle, and can take several hours to complete, and a modified version of Cranium Cariboo (www.boardgamegeek.com/boardgame/5718, accessed 2009), which works with letters, numbers, and counting.

Diana developed a low-cost gaming program for students to practice their skills. The fact that she paired traditional and perhaps not so traditional methods shows that she wasn't doing gaming in the classroom for the sake of making it available, but was strategically using the games as they fit the topic at hand. Incorporating a pastime Diana knew her students were interested in went a long way toward motivating them to learn. Diana states, "When I asked for mid-session and end-of-session feedback in their journals specific to the lessons, the majority of the group stated that they enjoyed summer school a lot more than they thought they would. They said that even though there was a lot of work to do every day, they learned a lot" (e-mail interview, August 2009).

▶ ORGANIZE A GAMING CAREER NIGHT

Gaming in an Academic Library: Gaming Career Night

The University of Illinois at Urbana-Champaign held a Gaming Career Night in 2009, organized by David Ward, Head of Information Services at the Undergraduate Library. While the university doesn't offer a gaming degree or a specific gaming curriculum, it does have a highly ranked engineering and computer science program and a growing collection of games at the Undergraduate Library (see Figure 5.1).

The university attracts many students interested in turning their college experience into a career in the gaming industry. In late 2005, the University of Illinois Library started a gaming initiative (www.library.illinois.edu/gaming, accessed 2009), which includes developing a gaming collection (current and historical) and programs and information resources to help students conduct research on and learn more about all aspects of gaming. In April

▶ Figure 5.1: Screenshot for Gaming Collection at the University of Illinois Undergraduate Library

2009 the library hosted a Gaming Career Night. The main goals of the program included:

- ▶ Informing students about requirements and best practices for getting careers in the gaming industry
- ▶ Creating information resources related to careers in the gaming industry
- ▶ Developing contacts and building relationships within the campus advisor and career counseling communities as well as the gaming industry

The panelists included programmers, artists, writers, project managers, and publicists. The discussion ranged from the day-to-day work expectations in a gaming company to ways to prepare portfolios of works for interviews to what classes and work experience were recommended to help build needed skills.

The panelists talked about how they got their start in the industry, interviewing tips, the role of a portfolio in the job search process, college classes helpful for gaming careers, and the role of internships and other work experience in preparing one for a career in gaming. In addition to the panelists, members of the local campus community, including the campus career center and academic advisors from departments related to gaming, attended.

Members of Volition (www.volition-inc.com, accessed 2009), a local gaming company, were also available to answer a wide range of student questions about how they could prepare themselves for a career in the gaming industry. Discussions included availability of local classes and other opportunities for gathering the kinds of experience discussed by Volition. Campus groups also demonstrated games they had created and sought critique from the Volition staff. A Web site (http://uiuc.libguides.com/ gamingcareers, accessed 2009) was created as a follow-up resource for students interested in pursuing these careers.

The event lasted about three hours. The first two hours included the panel discussion and an open question-and-answer session. The final hour consisted of the panelists talking individually to students, the student game demos, and Volition members demonstrating some of their upcoming games.

Marketing for the program consisted of the following:

▶ Flyers in the library, campus student union, and major classroom buildings in the engineering quad
▶ Facebook press release, targeting student gaming groups on Facebook, as well as a press release on the library's own Facebook page (www.facebook.com/group.php?gid=2212326596, accessed 2009)
▶ Blog post on the library's events blog (www.library.illinois.edu/ugl, accessed 2009)
▶ Signage and PA announcements in the library
▶ Press release to student and local community newspapers
▶ Press release sent out by campus advisers and career center to their students

Because not every university or library will have a gaming company in its town, a great resource to tap into is the International Game Developers Association (www.igda.com, accessed 2009). The association has local chapters and is made up of a network of people involved in the gaming industry field—not just game designers. It has a forums board where you can post to see if anyone is in your area and might be interested in speaking to students or patrons about their career. Many times those in the industry are contractors and may live quite a distance from the company they actually work for. Chances are you'll find someone not too far from your library who may be willing to come and speak. An online conference may be an option as well.

Because gaming is extremely interdisciplinary, computer science/engineering, art, math, writing, and theater are all departments to consider involving in such a career fair. If possible, schedule a time at the event for the experts to meet with the students one on one. The questions for the panelists were discussed before the actual event. Talking to student groups and those interested in gaming careers to find out what they want to know prior to the event can help make it successful for all.

▶ SUPPORT GAMING GROUPS FOR ALL AGES

Gaming in a Public Library: All Ages

Richard Glady, Library Assistant with the Scottsdale Public Library System in Arizona (http://library.ci.scottsdale.az.us, accessed 2009), started an Adult Gamers Group at the Civic Center Library. The Adult Gamers Group was meant to be a roped-off area for those 18 and older to play *Halo* on Xbox 360 and the online virtual worlds of Second Life and World of Warcraft. Based on the patrons who attended for six months from December 2007 through May 2008, he later changed it to all ages.

Because the management team in Youth Services initially opposed gaming, Richard brought his personal PS2 and then his Wii on the weekends so that he could run a small program for everyone. He also brought in some handheld devices, including the PlayStation Portable (PSP) and Nintendo DS. It's not uncommon for employees at libraries to bring their own gaming systems to get things started. He was later asked to run an adult gaming program by the library director when he started working in Adult Services.

Once naysayers see positive results, they will often decide to invest more time and money into gaming as a regular service. Fortunately this was the case for Richard at his library. He says, "There is strong commitment in our Strategic Plan to help our customers learn about new technology. Because I have tried several different types of consoles available I was able to help customers learn by playing with them" (e-mail interview, August 2009). It took about six months, but every library in the Scottsdale Public Library system now has a gaming program for tweens.

Although the event was advertised to run for three hours, it was usually set up by the time the library opened and packed up an hour before the library closed. It was held in a large open room where art was displayed. There were no other activities in the room at the time aside from the video gaming. Some of the games and consoles included *Guitar Hero* for the PS2 (because it was popular), *Rock Band* for PS3 (because it was new and kids of all ages can play it), *Wii Sports* (small learning curve), and *Viva Piñata* for Xbox 360 (games for all ages are hard to come by for the Xbox 360). There were over 1,100 attendees during the six months. In looking at some of the successes of the program beyond attendance, Richard notes that, "games are the great equalizer." He cites examples of teens who would help younger kids, and older adults, while still somewhat reluctant, would play as well. Richard felt that gaming brought in people different from those who regularly visit the library. The program also brought together strangers and families in good fun.

While he was able to set up, run, and take down the program as a one-man show, and eventually get some staff buy-in for other gaming programs throughout the system, there was still a disconnect between staff seeing the validity of offering gaming as a service in the library. It is important for administrators to help support such programs through inviting other staff to participate and to become familiar with the technology. Conversations around the relationship of gaming to literacy, skill building, and the library's strategic plan can go a long way to gaining support for gaming as a service. Richard was definitely the catalyst for his community when it came to introducing video games to his library system.

▶ LEARN FROM THE BEST PRACTICES OF OTHER LIBRARIANS

Games have circulated at the Park Ridge Public Library in Illinois (www.parkridgelibrary.org, accessed 2009) since February 2006. According to Maggie Hommel, who was the Young Adult Librarian at that time, hands down, the key to the continued success of the gaming collection was getting patron input from the start: "Paying attention to what the community wants is a great way to build a basis for the collection" (e-mail/phone interview, June 2009). For users who may not feel engaged in the library, asking for their input through a survey (see Figure 5.2, pp. 100–103) can be a great way for them to have a voice at the library.

Because there was also initially quite a bit of resistance from library administration to the idea of circulating games, getting input from the community of what is popular and building the collection in that direction proved useful. Gaming programs, including Scratch Academy (http://scratch.mit.edu, accessed 2009), which is a game design and animation program, is also offered at the Park Ridge Public Library and helped boost interest and support in having the collection. A list of the video games in the Park Ridge collection and the patron survey are available online (www.parkridgelibrary.org/movies_and_music/videogames .aspx, accessed 2009).

Todd Krueger, Collection Development Librarian at the Baltimore Public Library in Maryland (www.bcplonline.org, accessed 2009), began circulating games in summer 2006. He said that while there wasn't a whole lot of resistance to the idea from administrators, there were a few questions regarding the relationship of circulating games to the mission of the library as well as taxpayer dollars being spent on the collection. What helped Todd be able to make the idea a reality was that a neighboring library system was successfully circulating games. Paying attention to what your community is already doing can sometimes prove helpful! Todd also said that theft of the games was initially a larger issue than anticipated. "There was an incredible amount of theft. Even with safety features such as security cases tagged with RFID technologies, customers found a way around it. Much of the theft was due to people checking out the materials using multiple library cards and simply not returning the item. Fortunately the administration did not want to discontinue the collection" (phone interview, June 2009).

As a response, Todd said the library made the collection "reserve only." Customers are required to request the material via their library card, the premise being that the library will have a lot of contact information on the patrons before they check out the item(s). This seems to be working well for the Baltimore Public Library as an answer to the theft problem.

For one more look at a library that circulates video games (since 2004), we turn to John Scalzo, Librarian at the Irondequoit Public Library in Rochester, New York (www.libraryweb.org/irondequoit, accessed 2009). John has chronicled his library's foray into circulating video games through the Video Gaming Librarian column on Gaming Target (www.gamingtarget.com/articles.php?kywrd =The+Video+Game+Librarian, accessed 2009). A best practice John has to offer is to develop the collection carefully. "Both Metacritic (www.metacritic.com, accessed 2009) and Game Rankings (www.gamerankings.com accessed 2009) are godsends. The two sites give a real good idea of what the gaming community at large thinks of a certain game" (Meebo chat interview, June 2009). Pairing this information with input from the local community is a surefire way to start building a successful collection.

For an extensive list of best practices for gaming programs throughout the United States, visit the American Library Association's online gaming toolkit (www.librarygamingtoolkit.org/models.html, accessed 2009).

▶ DEVELOP YOUR OWN BEST PRACTICES

Hopefully the scenarios described in this chapter have given you some food for thought when it comes to developing your own gaming programs. The mechanics of each organization are going to be slightly different, and you can see from the examples that it's not always smooth sailing. Starting out what might seem to be small can be its own best practice. Growing the program by getting more staff on board and increasing funding if possible are key. Building gaming into the framework of the library's strategic goals and plan is important to helping making the program sustainable. All of this won't necessarily happen overnight. Taking time periodically to evaluate the program will go a long way toward building the foundation for this valuable service. Effective means of evaluation are described in the next chapter.

▶ Figure 5.2: Final YA Video Game Report

The two-year trial period for the Young Adult video game collection is now coming to an end. The collection has grown to 269 games, and includes PlayStation 3 and Wii games in addition to the original collection of Xbox 360, Xbox, and PlayStation 2 games. Circulation of the collection has continued to be very high, and response to the collection is overwhelmingly positive. Video game offerings now include a Children's and upcoming Adult/High School collection. Via the survey and purchase requests, patrons continue to ask for more games, handheld console games such as PSP and Nintendo DS, duplicate copies of popular games, and a greater overall selection.

Since the video game collection was started:

- Circulation of young adult books has increased nearly 51 percent (Chart 1).
- New YA patrons have begun using the Library, and existing YA patrons use the Library more frequently (Chart 2).
- Staff report that more teenage boys are being served in the YA Loft.
- There are nearly 150 more teen library card holders than there were in 2006.
- Circulation of YA video games continues to increase (Chart 3).

Video Game Survey:

123 responses as of February 13, 2008

Summary of results:

- When asked about usage of the YA Loft, 42 percent of respondents say they used the YA Loft weekly before the video game collection and 65 percent say they used the Loft weekly now.
- Nearly 60 percent of respondents check out books and video games when they visit the library, with just 5 percent saying they check out only video games.
- Recent comments from the video game survey:
  "Good but needs PSP games."
  "It's kind of awesome. And I'm going to check out Wii games."
  "It's good but it needs more games."
  "More titles."
  "It's great! Keep it up!"
  "It's OK. There are a lot of good games on the list, but it seems like you only have 1 copy of each title . . . all of the good games are usually checked out."

Future goals for the collection:

- Establish a budget for the video games.
- Continue to develop newer collections, such as PS3, Wii, and Xbox 360.
- Focus the collection on Teen titles, because Children's will be buying games for younger audience.
- Feature more duplicate copies of popular games and continue responding to requests.
- Keep up with new consoles, games, and trends.
- Support collection with programming.

(continued)

(continued)

Chart 1:
Young Adult Monthly Book Circulation
(YA Video Game collection started February 2006)

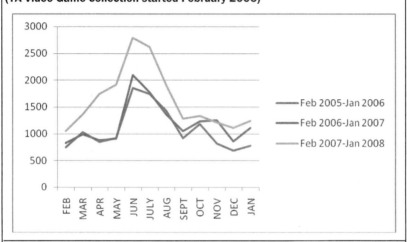

	FEB	MAR	APR	MAY	JUN	JUL	AUG	SEP	OCT	NOV	DEC	JAN
Feb 2005-Jan 2006	746	1,031	851	923	1,856	1,743	1,432	914	1,183	815	687	778
Feb 2006-Jan 2007	826	992	873	909	2,096	1,774	1,358	1,047	1,229	1,254	861	1,111
Feb 2007-Jan 2008	1,052	1,367	1,744	1,915	2,793	2,622	1,922	1,283	1,333	1,216	1,110	1,241

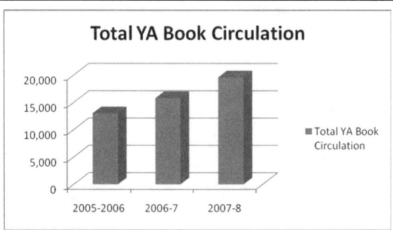

(continued)

(continued)

Annual Young Adult Book Circulation

Date range	Book circulation	% change from previous years
Feb 2005-Jan 2006	12,959	
Feb 2006-Jan 2007	14,330	Up **11%** from 2005-2006
Feb 2007-Jan 2008	19,598	Up **37%** from 2006-2007, Up **51%** from 2005-2006

Chart 2

How often did/do you come to the Library:

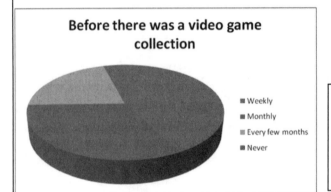

Before there was a video game collection

- Weekly
- Monthly
- Every few months
- Never

Weekly 42.1%
Monthly 32.6%
Every few months 21.1%
Never 4.2%

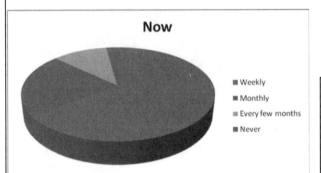

Now

- Weekly
- Monthly
- Every few months
- Never

Weekly 64.8%
Monthly 22%
Every few months 11%
Never 2.2%

(continued)

(continued)

Chart 3: YA Video Game Circulation

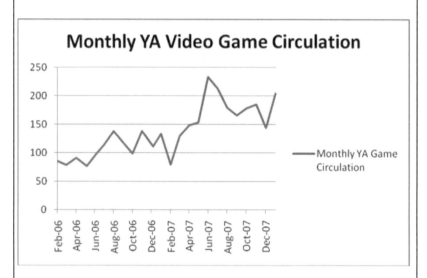

Monthly YA Video Game Circulation

*Note: Collection circulatiion spikes occurred when new games were added.

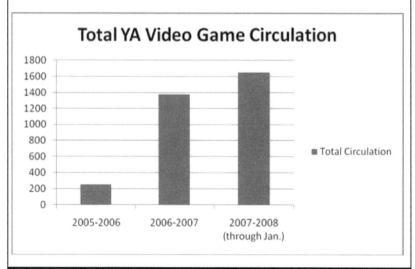

Total YA Video Game Circulation

	2005-2006	2006-2007	2007-2008 (through Jan)
Total Circulation	253	1,378	1,654

►6

MEASURES OF SUCCESS

► Use a Mixture of Measures
► Don't Focus Solely on Numbers
► Develop Outcomes
► Use Surveys as Evaluation Tools
► Reevaluate and Move Forward

Assessing the success of a program is important for building sustainability. The nature and complexity of your evaluation process will depend on the scope of your program. New gaming programs are often part of a larger program to target a specific age group or achieve a specific library goal. In either case, information regarding successful implementation and achievement of program objectives is important to record, especially when it comes time to apply for more funding.

► USE A MIXTURE OF MEASURES

Take surveys—whether formal or informal—at the end of your events to get feedback from the participants. If your library policy allows, take photos and videos. Also, keep these questions in mind; their answers will give you some key indicators of success:

► Are new people showing up and participating?
► What kind of mentorship is taking place among the players and/ or organizers?
► Are players involved in advertising and promotion?

▶ What are the connections among the participants and other library programs and services and even behavior?

Here are some further questions to examine based on specific game types:

▶ Monthly video game tournaments
  ➤ Are the tournament rules fair? If not, what would you adjust?
  ➤ Is the competition too hard, too easy, or just right?
▶ Board games
  ➤ Do people bring their own games and contribute to developing or judging the rules for the event?
  ➤ If there is alignment with the school curriculum and your board game tournament, do you notice changes in attitudes about schoolwork or other positive behaviors?
▶ *Magic: The Gathering*
  ➤ What is the progression of new players in terms of socialization?
▶ *Guitar Hero*
  ➤ Is there any visible transference in skills or interest in music creation at the library?
  ➤ What is the connection between the participants and other library programs and services?
▶ Anime fest
  ➤ Are new people showing up at related library events such as a manga club?
  ➤ Is circulation of related materials increasing?

▶ DON'T FOCUS SOLELY ON NUMBERS

No matter what type of program you have or which age group you target, there are two key points to keep in mind. The first point is that the success of a program should be judged on more than just the number of people who attend.

I will never forget a presentation by young adult author and librarian Patrick Jones, who discussed an example of a book club meeting where about 15 teens showed up. Not everyone was able to express their opinions at that particular meeting because some people talked constantly, so the program wasn't successful for all even though the numbers looked good on paper.

Library administrators may be very concerned with or seemingly overly focused on the numbers, particularly if they are facing budget restrictions. The first follow-up question with regard to a program might be something like, "how many people attended?" or this question might be the first answer when asked, "how did the program go?" While we're not going to get away from the fact that we usually have to count attendance no matter what because we are in the business of serving the community, there are fortunately other areas to consider to help paint the bigger picture of whether or not a program was successful. The bottom line is to try not to sweat it too much or to take it personally if your actual turnout does not equal your expected turnout. There could be literally a hundred different reasons why, including the weather, the time of day, or the marketing of the program.

The second key point to keep in mind is related to the first. Remember that it will take time to build an audience and interest in the program as well as meet your goals. "Time" can mean anywhere from several months to several years. Again, it might feel uncomfortable to be in a situation where you feel completely responsible for the number of people who show up or don't show up. You know that funds are not growing on the trees outside the library, and yet you want to explain how you need more time for the program to make an impact when it seems like the plug is going to be pulled at any moment. Albert Einstein once said that insanity is "doing the same thing over and over again and expecting different results," and we definitely don't want to be stuck in that place when we have the program again.

We also don't want to be stuck in a place where we're too fearful of having the program again or can't articulate why we should have had it in the first place. We all know as well that if we have a goal such as helping develop a more literate community, a one-shot program isn't going to begin to scratch the surface, at least not by itself. This is where evaluation comes in to determine what happened, how to make things different next time, and how to start connecting the pieces to form the bigger picture of meeting large library goals.

▶ DEVELOP OUTCOMES

You may feel like you barely have enough time to plan what seem to be the basics of the program, like how you are going to possibly have time to get off the reference desk so that you can be there when it takes place, much less think about developing outcomes for it. However, if you skip this step, you and other staff may be likely to slip into that narrow focus of believing that attendance is the only measure of success. If you look just at the number of people served and the amount of money spent, you're not really getting at the real impact the program had. Note that attendance and financial measures are considered outputs rather than outcomes. The difference is that outputs are library/organization centered while outcomes are patron focused.

Yes, developing outcomes does add one more thing to your already full plate, but, if it will help bring meaning to what you're doing by showing the impact and difference you're making, then it's also a great incentive to at least try to understand the process and start creating some more useful measures. Outcomes also help us keep in touch with our patrons' needs. We might think we know, and often we're correct, but we're also helping build a foundation of how to assess the impact our programs are making for when we specifically will no longer be with the organization.

Coming up with a few outcomes does not have to be a long drawn out, scary, and formalized process. In fact, you're more likely to be open to what outcomes may be possible at the point when the program is in its developing stages rather than at the moment when the patrons are lined up outside the door waiting for the program to start. Think back to the context of why the ideas for the program came about in the first place. Often those initial discussions included what the outcomes were to be.

For example, you may have had a staff meeting to brainstorm how to target a particular audience. Because you had heard about other libraries having success with a particular audience related to a gaming program, you thought it might be a great idea for your library to try it as well. One outcome might then be that members from the targeted audience who seldom go to the library attended the gaming event and even contributed ideas toward further developing the program for the future. You will also want to know how they became aware of the program for future marketing methods. Perhaps it was through a community agency that works with that particular audience. Raising awareness among others about your library programs is definitely a viable outcome and can be a building block to help develop future partners and programs.

What Do Outcomes Look Like?

An outcome should be measurable. "I would like to have five photos from the event that show library users interacting with one another" is a quantifiable task. "I would like to have memories from the event" needs to be a little more concrete. An outcome should incorporate the larger goals of the library as well. For example, if your program is meant to contribute toward developing the participants' literacy skills, you'll want to focus on those skills when summarizing the program for your reports and sharing anecdotes.

It's helpful to have the desirable outcomes on paper before the program begins. Otherwise, a likely scenario is that you'll be concentrating so much on some other aspect—like crowd control—you might forget what it is you're aiming for! Often there is only one person available to run the program, and immediate needs such as getting the technology to work might be a little more pressing than being able to thoughtfully observe how other parts of the program are going. However, give it your best shot.

Some examples of outcomes for your gaming program might look like the following:

> ▶ Participants explore what services the library has to offer (pick up a flyer, tell someone about a program or service, or browse materials during the program).
> ▶ Participants use a variety of information resources to instruct their game play (strategy guides, Internet, etc.).
> ▶ Participants interact with others they may not have met before the program.

▶ Participants mentor others at the program on how to use library resources relevant to the program.

▶ Participants contribute ideas or time to further developing the program (share equipment, help videotape the program, help advertise, etc.)

▶ Participants can articulate how the game they designed is played.

▶ Participants teach others how to play or create a game.

▶ Participants help promote the event by creating a short promotional video.

Outcomes can be short term, mid range, or long term depending on the type of program you are running. As mentioned earlier, even if it is a one-shot program, chances are it's related to a larger goal within your library system, so it's still important to gather any feedback from observations, anecdotes, and surveys that you can.

▶ USE SURVEYS AS EVALUATION TOOLS

Surveys can provide some insight into the impact the program had on the participants. Keep in mind that you probably won't get a lot of real in-depth answers, especially if the survey is something you hand out as the program is ending, when people are eager to catch their rides. Keep the survey short. Five to six questions is a good range to stay within.

Surveys can be handed out as part of the program or can be administered online through a free service such as Survey Monkey (www.surveymonkey.com, accessed 2009). Small incentives to fill out the survey, such as a random drawing to play a particular game of choice at the program, may get more people to fill it out. Letting people know what you will do with the information from the surveys can help them understand that the information they are providing is useful. Otherwise, if they think their answers won't matter, they will be less likely to want to fill anything out.

Examples of some questions you might consider including as part of your survey are as follows:

▶ Did you try something new that you hadn't done before? If so, what?

▶ Did you meet people you didn't know before the event?

▶ How long did you stay?

▶ If the library had a similar event in the future, would you invite your friends to come?

▶ Did you learn something new about the library? If so, what?

▶ On a scale of 1 to 5 (1 being the least), how much fun did you have? Explain.

▶REEVALUATE AND MOVE FORWARD

Outcomes and surveys are important tools to help you evaluate your program. As the saying goes, hindsight is always 20/20. Try to take some time by yourself after the program to assess what worked, what didn't work, and what could be done differently. The more you don't take things personally if nothing seemed to go right, the more you reach out to others to get their perspectives (including staff and patrons), the closer you'll be to heading in the right direction for improvement the next time around. Here are some questions to ask yourself:

▶ Did I try to take on too much myself, or did the workload seem about right?

▶ How do I feel about the marketing and promotion of the program?

▶ Do I feel the program matched the expectations of those who attended?

▶ Would community partnerships enhance the sustainability and quality of the program?

▶ Did the program reach the intended audience? If not, what might I try differently?

Finally, use a checklist similar to the one provided in Figure 6.1 to help you critically evaluate your program.

Evaluating your programs will help you improve your service to your patrons. Don't worry about whether or not you're doing it "right" from the get-go. You'll learn. The fact that you're trying to integrate program evaluations into your already hectic schedule is definitely a step in the right direction!

▶ Figure 6.1: Sample Self-Checklist for Evaluating Your Program

• *Use this checklist to help develop an effective process for evaluating a gaming program at your library.*

❏ Was my marketing as effective as it could have been? Where and how could I market the program next time?

_____

_____

❏ Was the attendance what I expected?

❏ Did I talk with my patrons before and during the program to get them interested and involved?

❏ Did I have staff buy-in and support? What might I do differently next time to get more staff support and promotion?

❏ _____

❏ Were the games of interest to the participants?

❏ Did I reach out to community organizations for support?

❏ Did I have a variety of activities available?

❏ Was the location a good one for the participants?

❏ Did I have the equipment I needed and working as I wanted it to?

❏ Did I prepare for the unexpected?

❏ What are some ways I might grow and expand the program?

    Different games? _____

    More than games? _____

    Outreach opportunities? _____

    Patron input? _____

▶

REFERENCES AND
RECOMMENDED RESOURCES

▶ ONLINE RESOURCES

If you want to find the most up-to-date information on a topic, your first choice for information might not be to consult a book. This is probably even more so regarding the topic of technology and, specifically, video games. By the time many gaming magazines are catalogued and hit the library shelves, they are yesterday's news. We often turn to online resources to catch the most recent information about gaming, whether it be reviews, summaries from a recent convention, or daily blog posts from the trend spotters who are in the trenches, delivering the information to us at the convenience of our computer.

While I'll include resources specific to trends, upcoming features and games for consoles, handhelds, and computers, and board and card games later in this chapter, I'll begin with a list of some broader online resources that deal with gaming in general. While the list isn't comprehensive, it is a place to start for an overview. First I want to mention these good resources for librarians: LibSuccess wiki (www.libsuccess.org, accessed 2009), LibGaming Google Group (http://groups.google.com/group/LibGaming, accessed 2009), ALA Connect (http://connect.ala.org, which has a Games and Gaming group at http://connect.ala.org/gaming, accessed 2009), and John Scalzo's Video Game Librarian blog (www.videogamelibrarian.com, accessed 2009). There is also a companion wiki for this book, and References and Recommended Readings are included as the final section of this chapter.

Board Game Geek (www.boardgamegeek.com): Reviews and forums board for board and card games.

Board Games with Scott (www.boardgameswithscott.com): Video reviews of board games by librarian Scott Nicholson.

CosPlay Lab (www.cosplaylab.com): Resources and galleries for costumes inspired by anime, manga, and related gaming media.

The Escapist (www.escapistmagazine.com): Articles and columns regarding video gaming culture.

Gamasutra (www.gamasutra.com): Video game news and resources for game developers.

GameFAQs (www.gamefaqs.com): Walk throughs and reviews for video games.

Games in Libraries (www.gamesinlibraries.org): Monthly podcast, usually by librarians, on a variety of topics related to board, card, and video games.

GameSpot (www.gamespot.com): Reviews and news for almost all video gaming platforms.

Game Studies (http://gamestudies.org/0801): International journal on computer game research.

Game Trailers (www.gametrailers.com): Game trailers, recorded game play, and reviews.

Gaming in Libraries course (http://gamesinlibraries.org/course): Video-based course on gaming in libraries by Scott Nicholson with Syracuse University.

G4 TV (http://g4tv.com): Video news and previews on the world of video gaming.

IGN (www.ign.com): Game guides, news, and reviews.

International Journal for the Study of Board Games (www .boardgamestudies.info/studies): An academic journal for historical and systematic research regarding board games.

Joystiq (www.joystiq.com): Video gaming blog and podcast.

KoinUp (www.koinup.com): Photos, screenshots, and machinima for virtual worlds.

Kotaku (http://kotaku.com): Reviews, previews, and latest news on video games.

Librarian's Guide to Gaming (http://librarygamingtoolkit.org): American Library Association and Verizon resource for board, card, and video games.

Mario Brothers Memorial Public Library (www.mbmpl.org): Resource for librarians, written by librarian Jami Schwarzwalder, on video and tabletop games, virtual worlds, and collection development for games.

Massively (www.massively.com): News about massively multiplayer online role-playing games.

1UP.com (www.1up.com): Game reviews, news, and podcasts.

Penny Arcade (www.penny-arcade.com): Webcomic on video games and gaming culture.

Rezed (www.rezed.org): Resources and research for those using virtual worlds for learning.

Unfiction (www.unfiction.com): Alternate reality game resource including current games and forums boards.

▶TRENDS

Why should a library keep abreast of gaming trends? Most libraries don't have the funding for the latest and greatest. One reason is that it will help get your mental wheels turning for partnership ideas and grant-funded projects. The knowledge you might gain from knowing what is up and coming can also help you decide what to budget your gaming monies on, especially if something seems to fit within your library's strategic plan.

The annual E3 Expo (www.e3expo.com, accessed 2009) is an excellent resource for information about trends in gaming. E3 is the Electronic Entertainment Expo. It is a trade show for computer and video games. This is where the major companies, such as Microsoft, Sony, and Nintendo, announce their upcoming products. While attendance is restricted to those within the industry, many of the above-listed online resources will report highlights from the Expo.

The Library Gaming Census reports by Scott Nicholson (at Syracuse University) can help identify what role gaming is playing in services at public, school, and academic libraries. The 2006 and 2007 reports are available, and 2008 was expected in late 2009 but was not yet available at the time of this writing. The data collection team at Syracuse University looks at what goals libraries are aiming toward and makes the information accessible for those creating gaming guides for libraries based on who they want to target and what goals they want to reach. The censuses can be found online at the Library Game Lab of Syracuse (http://gamelab.syr.edu, accessed 2009) by selecting the "Publications" link.

The MacArthur Foundation (www.macfound.org, accessed 2009), while not focusing solely on gaming, has earmarked $50 million for digital media and learning (http://digitallearning .macfound.org/site/c.enJLKQNlFiG/b.2029199/k.94AC/Latest_ News.htm, accessed 2009) for a five-year stretch beginning in 2006 "to help determine how digital technologies are changing the way young people learn, play, socialize, and participate in civic life." A lot of the projects that have been funded by MacArthur through these monies are related to gaming. This is a great resource to learn about what digital media means for youth and learning. Studying the connection between games and learning is a large part of the initiative.

▶ BOARD GAMES AND CARD GAMES

For up-to-date reviews on board games for libraries, including number of players, content, and length of play, Scott Nicholson's video blog (www.boardgameswithscott.com, accessed 2009) is a fantastic resource. Scott is an author, associate professor, and Program Director for the Library and Information Science program at Syracuse University and runs the Game Lab at the school.

The Library Gaming blog (http://librarygamer.wordpress .com, accessed 2009) by Brian Mayer, Library Technology Specialist with the School Library System of the Genesee Valley BOCES, has up-to-date recommendations for board and card games that particularly tie in with the New York State school curriculum and the American Association of School Librarians *Standards for the 21st-Century Learner* (www.ala.org/ala/mgrps/divs/aasl/ guidelinesandstandards/learningstandards/standards.cfm, accessed 2009). Also, check out the book *Libraries Got Game: Aligned Learning Through Modern Board Games*, written by Brian Mayer and Christopher Harris (ALA Editions, 2009).

▶ REFERENCES AND RECOMMENDED READING

Books

Beck, John C. 2006. *The Kids Are Alright: How the Gamer Generation Is Changing the Workplace.* Boston: Harvard Business School Press.

Edery, David and Ethan Mollik. 2009. *Changing the Game: How Video Games Are Transforming the Future of Business.* Upper Saddle River, NJ: FT Press.

Gallaway, Beth. 2009. *Game On! Gaming at the Library.* New York: Neal-Schuman.

Gee, James Paul. 2007. *Good Video Games and Good Learning: Collected Essays on Video Games, Learning, and Literacy (New Literacies and Digital Epistemologies).* New York: Peter Lang.

———. 2007. *What Video Games Have to Teach Us about Learning and Literacy,* 2nd ed. New York: Palgrave Macmillan.

Goodstein, Anastasia. 2007. *Totally Wired: What Teens and Tweens Are Really Doing Online.* New York: St. Martin's Griffin.

Harris, Amy, and Scott Rice. 2008. *Gaming in Academic Libraries: Collections, Marketing, and Information Literacy.* Chicago: Association of College and Research Libraries.

Hutchison, David. 2007. *Playing to Learn: Video Games in the Classroom.* Santa Barbara: Libraries Unlimited.

Johnson, Steven. 2006. *Everything Bad Is Good for You: How Today's Popular Culture Is Actually Making Us Smarter.* New York: Riverhead Trade.

Kutner, Lawrence, and Cheryl Olson. 2008. *Grand Theft Childhood: The Surprising Truth about Violent Video Games and What Parents Can Do.* New York: Simon & Schuster.

Levine, Jenny. 2006. *Gaming & Libraries Update: Intersection of Services*, vol. 42, no. 5. Chicago: ALA TechSource.

————. 2008. *Gaming & Libraries Update: Broadening the Intersections*, vol. 44, no. 3. Chicago: ALA TechSource.

————. 2009. *Gaming & Libraries: Learning Lessons from the Intersections*, vol. 45, no. 5. Chicago: ALA TechSource.

Mayer, Brian, and Christopher Harris. 2009. *Libraries Got Game: Aligned Learning Through Modern Board Games*. Chicago: ALA Graphics.

Neiburger, Eli. 2009. *Gamers . . . In the Library?! The Why, What, and How of Video Game Tournaments for All Ages*. Chicago: ALA Editions.

Prensky, Marc. 2006. *Don't Bother Me Mom—I'm Learning! How Computer and Video Games Are Preparing Your Kid for Twenty-First-Century Success and How You Can Help*. St. Paul: Paragon House.

Magazines and Journals

"Big Book of FREE: Special Collector's Edition." August 2009. *PC Gamer.* Available: www.pcgamer.com (accessed 2009).

Davis, Craig, Christy Mulligan, and Rick Kelsey. 2007. "From Playing to Creating: Teaching Game Design to Children and Teens." *School Library Journal* (October 1). Available: www.schoollibrary journal.com/article/CA6484337.html (accessed 2009).

Eastwood, Lori, and Lindsay Patrick Wesson. 2009. "Gamers Are Readers: Capitalize on the Popularity of Video Games." *School Library Journal* (April 1). Available: www.schoollibraryjournal .com/article/CA6647714.html (accessed 2009).

The Escapist. Available: www.escapistmagazine.com (accessed 2009).

Game Informer. Available: www.gameinformer.com (accessed 2009).

Game Pro. Available: www.gamepro.com (accessed 2009).

Helmrich, Erin, and Eli Neiburger. 2007. "Video Games as a Service: Three Years Later." *VOYA.* Available: http://pdfs.voya .com/VO/YA2/VOYA200706video_games.pdf (accessed 2009).

Nintendo Power. Available: www.nintendopower.com (accessed 2009).

Official Xbox Magazine. Available: www.oxmonline.com (accessed 2009).

PC Gamer. Available: www.pcgamer.com (accessed 2009).

Scordato, Julie. 2008. "Gaming as a Library Service." *Public Libraries*, no. 1 (January/February): 67–73.

Web Sites

Board Games and the American Association of School Libraries Standards for the 21st-Century Learner. 2008. School Library System of Genesee Valley BOCES. Available: http://sls.gvboces.org/gaming/node/23 (accessed 2009).

Gamasutra—The Art & Business of Making Games. Available: www.gamasutra.com (accessed 2009).

Games and Gaming Member Interest Group (MIG). 2009. American Library Association. Available: http://connect.ala.org/node/66247 (accessed 2009).

Games, Gamers, and Gaming. 2009. *Library Journal.* Available: www.libraryjournal.com (accessed 2009).

Games in Libraries. 2009. A podcast about Games, Gaming, and Gamers in Libraries. Available: www.gamesinlibraries.org (accessed 2009).

Gaming, Learning, and Libraries Symposium. 2007. ALA TechSource. Available: http://gaming.techsource.ala.org/index.php/2007_Symposium (accessed 2009).

———. 2008. ALA TechSource. Available: http://gaming.techsource.ala.org/index.php/Main_Page (accessed 2009).

IGN Entertainment Games. Available: www.ign.com (accessed 2009).

1UP.com. Available: www.1up.com (accessed 2009).

Joystiq. 2003. Available: www.joystiq.com (accessed 2009).

Kotaku, the Gamer's Guide. Available: www.kotaku.com (accessed 2009).

Lenhart, Amanda, et al. Gaming. Pew Internet & American Life. Available: www.pewinternet.org/topics/Gaming.aspx (accessed 2009).

LibGaming Google Groups. Available: http://groups.google
.com/group/LibGaming (accessed 2009).

The Librarian's Guide to Gaming: An Online Toolkit for Building
Gaming at Your Library. 2009. American Library Association.
Available: http://librarygamingtoolkit.org (accessed 2009).

National Gaming Day at the Library. American Library Association. Available: http://ngd.ala.org (accessed 2009).

Nicholson, Scott. Board Games with Scott. Available: www
.boardgameswithscott.com (accessed 2009).

———2009. Gaming in Libraries—The Course. Available: www
.gamesinlibraries.org/course (accessed 2009).

The Video Game Librarian. Available: www.videogamelibrarian
.com (accessed 2009).

INDEX

Page numbers followed by the letter "f" indicate figures.

ABOUT THE AUTHOR

Kelly Nicole Czarnecki is a Technology Education Librarian at ImaginOn (NC), the Public Library of Charlotte & Mecklenburg County. She was a Library Journal Mover and Shaker in 2007. She served on the expert gaming panel for ALA and the Verizon Foundation 2008–2009. She writes a column, the Gaming Life, for *School Library Journal.* She frequently speaks at conferences when she's not writing.